What the Anti-Federalists Were *For*

D0043226

THE UNIVERSITY OF WINNIPEG
LIBRARY

What the
Anti-Federalists Were
For

Herbert J. Storing

With the Editorial Assistance of Murray Dry

The University of Chicago Press

Chicago and London

This publication was made possible, in part, by grants from the Institute for Educational Affairs, the National Endowment for the Humanities, Project '87, and Natico, Inc.

The University of Chicago Press, Chicago 60637
The University of Chicago Press, Ltd., London

Library of Congress Cataloging in Publication Data

Storing, Herbert J., 1928–77
    What the Anti-Federalists were for.

    Introduction to the author's The complete Anti-Federalist.
    Bibliography: p.
    Includes index.
    1. United States—Constitutional history.
2. United States—Politics and government—1783–1789.
3. Political science—United States—History.
I. Dry, Murray. II. Title.
JK116.S8   342.73′024   81-11395
ISBN 0-226-77574-7 (pbk.) 347.30224   AACR2

Contents

Preface

In November 1963, Herbert J. Storing wrote to the University of Chicago Press, proposing an edition of Anti-Federalist writings. In 1977, he delivered *The Complete Anti-Federalist* to the Press. When Storing died, in September 1977, the copy editing had barely begun. In the spring of 1978 I was asked to assist the Press in bringing my former teacher's substantially completed manuscript to publication. I agreed to fill in all the cross references, check all the quotations and source citations, and read the proofs.

The aim of Storing's monumental work was, in his words, "to make available for the first time all of the substantial Anti-Federal writings in their complete original form and in an accurate text, together with appropriate annotation." In comprehensiveness and scholarly thoroughness it is unlikely ever to be superseded. (For contents, see below, pp. 101–6.)

What the Anti-Federalists Were For is Storing's introduction to the writings and appears in volume one of the full edition. Because it stands on its own as a splendid exposition of their thought, it was decided to issue it also as a separate paperback. Storing presents enough of the Federalist argument to explain precisely what the Anti-Federalists—the opponents of the Constitution—were *for,* and to make clear in what sense they too deserve to be counted among the Founding Fathers. He concludes that the Anti-Federalists lost the debate because they had the weaker argument; yet he also argues that their concerns and principles continue to play an important part in the dialogue over the life of the American polity.

Anti-Federalists are cited in the notes (pp. 79–100) by a three-part number, the first denoting the volume of *The Complete Anti-Federalist* in which the respective writing appears, the second the position of the essay or series within that volume, and the third the paragraph.

Murray Dry

Middlebury, Vermont
1981

What the Anti-Federalists Were *For*

I

Introduction

The Constitution of the United States was viewed by the founding generation as distinctive, even unique, in the extent to which it was the product of
deliberation. Most previous foundings seemed to have been the result of
chance or the edict of one all-powerful man. But the United States Constitution was framed by a numerous and diverse body of statesmen, sitting
for over three months; it was widely, fully, and vigorously debated in the
country at large; and it was adopted by (all things considered) a remarkably
open and representative procedure. Viewed in this light, those who opposed
the Constitution must be seen as playing an indispensable if subordinate part
in the founding process. They contributed to the dialogue of the American
founding. To take only the most obvious case, the Constitution that came
out of the deliberations of 1787 and 1788 was not the same Constitution that
went in; for it was accepted subject to the understanding that it would be
amended immediately to provide for a bill of rights. Moreover, the founding
of a nation does not end with the making of a constitution. The Constitution
did settle many questions, and it established a lasting structure of rules and
principles—we do not adopt the current cant that fundamental law is
shapeless stuff to be formed at will by future generations. But it did not
settle *everything;* it did not finish the task of making the American polity.
The political life of the community continues to be a dialogue, in which the
Anti-Federalist concerns and principles still play an important part.

The Anti-Federalists are entitled, then, to be counted among the Founding Fathers, in what is admittedly a somewhat paradoxical sense, and to
share in the honor and the study devoted to the founding. In general,
however, they have not enjoyed such a position. Champions of a negative
and losing cause, they have found only a cramped place in the shadow of the
great constitutional accomplishment of 1787. They have often been presented as narrow-minded local politicians, unwilling to face the utter inadequacy of the Articles of Confederation or incapable of seeing beyond the
boundaries of their own states or localities. They have been described as
men without principle, willing to use any argument to drag down the Constitution, yet willing, many of them, when the Constitution was adopted, to
change their colors and become enthusiastic Federalists.[1] It is true that with
the rise of the Beardian critique of the Constitution and its framers, the
Anti-Federalists have been viewed with a more friendly eye. Merrill Jensen

3

has taught us to take seriously the possibility that the Anti-Federalists were right about the need for only modest changes in the Articles of Confederation and about the departure of the Constitution from the principles of the Revolution. He has inspired a full historical account of the Anti-Federal movement, and he has pointed to the need to take up the serious study of Anti-Federal thought. At the same time, the harsh edges of Beardian analysis have been worn away, and we are now in a position to consider afresh the class differences involved in the constitutional controversy, freed of many of the Beardian excesses.[2] Yet valuable as all of this has been, the corrected Beardian eye betrays still its original squint. It tends to see simple democratic agrarians among the Anti-Federalists as it tends to see self-seeking commercial oligarchs among the Federalists.[3] There is some basis for these views, but the picture is thin and distorted. Indeed, one of the few substantial accounts of Anti-Federal thought is a persuasive refutation of the Beardian thesis as applied to the Anti-Federalists and an attempt to show that the Anti-Federalists were in fact "men of little faith" in American national self-government.[4] Gordon Wood has added greatly to our understanding of the Anti-Federalists in his rich and encyclopedic account of the American founding and the way the Americans gradually blundered into a new political theory. Deep and lucid as his insights often are, however, Wood is finally less interested in understanding the Anti-Federalists (or the Federalists) as they understood themselves than in exposing the deeper social forces from which the whole sphere of "ideology," to use Bailyn's term, is derivative. Thus a debate that was for the Anti-Federalists fundamentally political becomes for Wood fundamentally sociological.[5]

There has been no sustained, comprehensive attempt to examine the thought, the principles, the argument of the Anti-Federalists, as they were understood by the Anti-Federalists themselves and by the other men of that time. Such an examination will be undertaken here. The aim will not be a history of the Anti-Federal movement or an analysis of its economic, sociological, or psychological underpinnings. We shall try to avoid presupposing some external set of questions or framework of analysis. Rather, we shall try to proceed from inside Anti-Federal thought, seeing the questions as they saw them, following the arguments as they made them. We shall explore the different levels of Anti-Federal theorizing, working our way critically through and if necessary beyond them, but always with the idea that the Anti-Federalists may have something to teach. Because the American founding took the form of a debate or dialogue, Anti-Federal thought is best examined within the movement and different levels of that dialogue. For this reason it will be necessary to take some note of the Federalist as well as the Anti-Federalist side of the debate, but the purpose is to present only so much of what the Anti-Federalists were against as is necessary to understand what they were for.

In beginning with the question of what the Anti-Federalists were *for*, we are not, it must be admitted, adhering to the aim of presenting the Anti-

Federalist argument as it presented itself. The Anti-Federalists were primarily *against* the Constitution. We do remain true to our aim in a deeper and more significant sense, however, because the Anti-Federalists themselves understood their negative conclusions about the Constitution to be derived from a positive political theory or set of political principles.*[6] The aim, then, will be to give a sympathetic, critical, and full account of the fundamental Anti-Federal position.

Was there, however, a single Anti-Federal position? In the most obvious sense there surely was not. The Federalists claimed that the opposers of the Constitution could not agree among themselves, that they shared no common principles, that their arguments canceled each other out. This is an exaggeration, for there was more agreement about many points of opposition to the Constitution than might appear at first glance.[7] Yet it is not possible to read far among the Anti-Federal writings without being struck by an extraordinary heterogeneity. It would be difficult to find a single point about which *all* of the Anti-Federalists agreed. They did not, finally, even agree unanimously in opposing the adoption of the Constitution. Many favored adoption if amendments could be secured; and others finally accepted the Constitution, even without a guarantee of amendment, as the best of the available choices. There is in fact no hard and fast way of even identifying "Anti-Federalists." Some men, notably Edmund ʹRandolph, were Federalist and Anti-Federalist at different times. Moderate or lukewarm adherents to either side were often almost indistinguishable from one another. Moreover, the specific points of disagreement and the reasons given by the Anti-Federalists were various and even contradictory. This is not to say that the Federalists were in much better condition. There is an impression of greater unity here because the Federalists were (in general) unified in supporting the Constitution, although some Federal reservations are scarcely distinguishable from Anti-Federal objections. That impression has been strengthened by the Federalists' victory and by the massive impact on later generations of *The Federalist* papers, which have tended to occupy the Federalist stage and lend their unity to the whole group supporting the Constitution.*[8] There were in fact diverse and contradictory opinions among the Federalists just as there were among their opponents.

If the Federalists and Anti-Federalists were divided among themselves, they were, at a deeper level, united with one another. Their disagreements were not based on different premises about the nature of man or the ends of political life. They were not the deep cleavages of contending regimes. They were the much less sharp and clear-cut differences within the family, as it were, of men agreed that the purpose of government is the regulation and thereby the protection of individual rights and that the best instrument for this purpose is some form of limited, republican government. It is their common ground that explains, to a large extent, the relatively unclear line

*References to substantive notes are accompanied by an asterisk.

between the two camps and the diversity within each of them. This is not to say that the differences are negligible, as those would argue who claim that there is no basic political controversy or political theorizing in the United States.⁹ The differences are limited, but they are nevertheless substantial and well formed. The nation was born in consensus but it lives in controversy, and the main lines of that controversy are well-worn paths leading back to the founding debate.

In searching for the underlying unity in the Anti-Federal position we are not tabulating the frequency of different arguments. We are looking not for what is *common* so much as for what is *fundamental*. We might well find the foundations laid in a very few writings, even a single one. Thus, on the Federalist side, a James Madison is more important in this kind of quest than a Tench Coxe, not because he is more typical or more influential in a direct sense but because he sees farther or better. He can *explain* more. The same is true on the Anti-Federal side of The Federal Farmer, Brutus, and such little known writers as A [Maryland] Farmer and The Impartial Examiner. Not all of these men were widely read, and some of them made arguments that were uncommon; but they explored or at least exposed the theoretical ground that most other Anti-Federalists took for granted.

Proceeding in this way, clearing our path through the superficial tangle, dealing as well as we can with the patches of obscurity and looseness we find in even the best Anti-Federal thinkers, we shall discover a set of principles that is a good deal clearer and more coherent, and also more relevant to an understanding of the American founding and the American polity, than has usually been supposed. But we shall also find, at the very heart of the Anti-Federal position, a dilemma or a tension. This is the critical weakness of Anti-Federalist thought and at the same time its strength and even its glory. For the Anti-Federalists could neither fully reject nor fully accept the leading principles of the Constitution. They were indeed open to Hamilton's scornful charge of trying to reconcile contradictions.¹⁰ This is the element of truth in Cecelia Kenyon's characterization of them as men of little faith. They did not fail to *see* the opportunity for American nationhood that the Federalists seized so gloriously, but they could not join in grasping it. They doubted; they held back; they urged second thoughts. This was, however, not a mere failure of will or lack of courage. They had *reasons,* and the reasons have weight. They thought—and it cannot easily be denied—that this great national opportunity was profoundly problematical, that it could be neither grasped nor let alone without risking everything. The Anti-Federalists were committed to both union and the states; to both the great American republic and the small, self-governing community; to both commerce and civic virtue; to both private gain and public good. At its best, Anti-Federal thought explores these tensions and points to the need for any significant American political thought to confront them; for they were not resolved by the Constitution but are inherent in the principles and traditions of American political life.

2
Conservatives

One of the striking and, to many readers, surprising aspects of the debate over the Constitution is the conservative posture of the opposition. The Anti-Federalists did not deny the need for some change, but they were on the whole defenders of the status quo. They deplored departures of the Constitution from "the good old way" or "the antient and established usage of the commonwealth." They shook their heads at "the phrenzy of innovation" sweeping the country: "The framing entirely new systems, is a work that requires vast attention; and it is much easier to guard an old one." They warned that constant change would leave Americans "always young in government."[1] Some expressed the primitive conservative view that whatever is old is good. Others revealed profound (but seldom explored) misgivings about the modern political principles on which the Constitution was so wholeheartedly based.*[2] Ordinarily, however, their conservatism was neither so shallow nor so deep. In the main, they saw in the Framers' easy thrusting aside of old forms and principles threats to four cherished values: to law, to political stability, to the principles of the Declaration of Independence, and to federalism.

The Anti-Federalists often objected even to entering into debate on the Constitution because of legal irregularities in the proceedings of the Philadelphia Convention. They argued that that Convention had been authorized "for the sole and express purpose of revising the Articles of Confederation," and had no right to propose any radical change in the government of the Union.[3] While not invincible, this argument is very powerful; but it became less pertinent every day simply because the Constitution was in fact before the people and its merits under discussion. The threshold had been crossed, and the Anti-Federalists had little choice but to follow the Federalists over it. But there were other legal objections. The Convention proposed that Congress and the state legislatures should be bypassed in favor of special ratifying conventions and that the Constitution should come into effect when nine states ratified. For neither of these proposals was there any legal basis. They ran counter to Congress's commission to the Convention, and they violated the mode of amendment established in the Articles of Confederation.

The proposals of the Framers were self-defeating in their casual disregard of the forms of legality: "the same reasons which you *now* urge for destroying our *present* federal government, may be urged for *abolishing the*

7

system which you now propose to adopt; and as the *method prescribed* by the *articles* of confederation is *now totally disregarded* by you, as *little regard* may be shewn by you to the *rules prescribed* for the amendment of the *new system. . . .*" "Charters," Rawlins Lowndes warned, "ought to be considered as sacred things. . . ." The Anti-Federalists saw in the proceedings and proposals of the Philadelphia Convention a threat to that "publick faith and confidence," which "bind[s] and cement[s] the community" and "establish[es] them as a body politick."[4] Of course the Anti-Federalists agreed that the people have a right to alter their governments; but they insisted that any revolution (including the one most of them had proudly aided) must be secured by an initially fragile political stability. They criticized the Federalists, in typical conservative fashion, for threatening this precious stability. "The late revolution having effaced in a great measure all former habits, and the present institutions are so recent, that there exists not that great reluctance to innovation, so remarkable in old communities, and which accords with reason, for the most comprehensive mind cannot foresee the full operation of material changes on civil polity. . . ." Hasty and blind adoption of government will lead to hasty and blind alterations, "and changes must ensue, one after another, till the peaceable and better part of the community will grow weary with changes, tumults and disorders, and be disposed to accept any government, however despotic, that shall promise stability and firmness."[5]

Far from straying from the principles of the American Revolution, as some of the Federalists accused them of doing,[6] the Anti-Federalists saw themselves as the true defenders of those principles. "I am fearful," said Patrick Henry, "I have lived long enough to become an old fashioned fellow: Perhaps an invincible attachment to the dearest rights of man, may, in these refined enlightened days, be deemed *old fashioned:* If so, I am contented to be so: I say, the time has been, when every pore of my heart beat for American liberty, and which, I believe, had a counterpart in the breast of every true American."[7] The Anti-Federalists argued, as some historians have argued since, that the Articles of Confederation were the constitutional embodiment of the principles on which the Revolution was based:

Sir, I venerate the spirit with which every thing was done at the trying time in which the Confederation was formed. America had then a sufficiency of this virtue to resolve to resist perhaps the first nation in the universe, even unto bloodshed. What was her aim? Equal liberty and safety. What ideas had she of this equal liberty? Read them in her Articles of Confederation.[8]

The innovators were impatient to change this "most excellent constitution," which was "sent like a blessing from heaven," for a constitution "essentially differing from the principles of the revolution, and from freedom," and thus destructive of the whole basis of the American community. "Instead of repairing the old and venerable fabrick, which sheltered the

United States, from the dreadful and cruel storms of a tyrannical British ministry, they built a stately palace after their own fancies. . . ."[9]

The principal characteristic of that "venerable fabrick" was its federalism: the Articles of Confederation established a league of sovereign and independent states whose representatives met in congress to deal with a limited range of common concerns in a system that relied heavily on voluntary cooperation. Federalism means that the states are primary, that they are equal, and that they possess the main weight of political power. The defense of the federal character of the American union was the most prominent article of Anti-Federalist conservative doctrine. While some of the other concerns were intrinsically more fundamental, the question of federalism was central and thus merits fuller discussion here, as it did in that debate.

To begin with an apparently small terminological problem, if the Constitution was opposed because it was anti-federal how did the opponents come to be called Anti-Federalists? They usually denied, in fact, that the name was either apt or just, and seldom used it themselves. They were, they often claimed, the true federalists. Some of them seemed to think that their proper name had been filched, while their backs were turned, as it were, by the pro-Constitution party, which refused to give it back; and versions of this explanation have been repeated by historians.[10] Unquestionably the Federalists saw the advantage of a label that would suggest that those who opposed the Constitution also opposed such a manifestly good thing as federalism. But what has not been sufficiently understood is that the term "federal" had acquired a specific ambiguity that enabled the Federalists not merely to take but to keep the name.

One of the perennial issues under the Articles of Confederation involved the degree to which the general government—or the instrumentality of the federation per se—was to be supported or its capacity to act strengthened. In this context one was "federal" or "anti-federal" according to his willingness or unwillingness to strengthen or support the institutions of the federation. This was James Wilson's meaning when he spoke of the "fœderal disposition and character" of Pennsylvania. It was Patrick Henry's meaning when he said that, in rejecting the Constitution, New Hampshire and Rhode Island "have refused to become federal." It was the meaning of the New York Assembly when in responding coolly to the recommendations of the Annapolis Convention it nevertheless insisted on its "truly federal" disposition.[11] This usage had thoroughly penetrated political discussion in the United States. In the straightforward explanation of Anti-Federalist George Bryan, "The name of Federalists, or Federal men, grew up at New York and in the eastern states, some time before the calling of the Convention, to denominate such as were attached to the general support of the United States, in opposition to those who preferred local and particular advantages.

9

. . ." Later, according to Bryan, "this name was taken possession of by those who were in favor of the new federal government, as they called it, and opposers were called Anti-Federalists."[12] Recognizing the pre-1787 usage, Jackson Turner Main tries, like Bryan, to preserve the spirit of Federalist larceny by suggesting that during the several years before 1787 "the men who wanted a strong national government, who might more properly be called 'nationalists,' began to appropriate the term 'federal' for themselves" and to apply the term "antifederal" to those hostile to the measures of Congress and thus presumably unpatriotic.*[13] But there was nothing exceptional or improper in the use of the term "federal" in this way; the shift in meaning was less an "appropriation" than a natural extension of the language, which the Federalists fully exploited.

The point of substance is that the Federalists had a legitimate *claim* to their name and therefore to their name for their opponents. Whether they had a better claim than their opponents cannot be answered on the basis of mere linguistic usage but only by considering the arguments. When, during the years of the Confederation, one was called a "federal man," his attachment to the principles of federalism was not at issue; that was taken for granted, and the point was that he was a man who (given this federal system) favored strengthening the "federal" or general authority. The ambiguity arose because strengthening the federal *authority* could be carried so far as to undermine the federal *principle;* and that was precisely what the Anti-Federalists claimed their opponents were doing.[14] Thus The Impartial Examiner argued that, despite the "sound of names" on which the advocates of the Constitution "build their fame," it is the opponents who act "on the broader scale of true *fœderal principles.*" They desire "a continuance of each distinct sovereignty—and are anxious for such a degree of energy in the general government, as will cement the union in the strongest manner."[15] It was possible (or so the Anti-Federalists believed) to be a federalist in the sense of favoring a strong agency of the federation and, at the same time, to be a federalist in the sense of adhering to the principle of a league of independent states.[16] In the name of federalism in the former sense, it was claimed, the proponents of the Constitution had abandoned federalism in the latter (and fundamental) sense.

The Anti-Federalists stood, then, for federalism in opposition to what they called the consolidating tendency and intention of the Constitution— the tendency to establish one complete national government, which would destroy or undermine the states.[17] They feared the implications of language like Washington's reference, in transmitting the Constitution to Congress, to the need for "the consolidation of our Union."[18] They saw ominous intentions in Publius' opinion that "a NATION, without a NATIONAL GOVERNMENT, is, in my view, an awful spectacle."[19] They resented and denied suggestions that "we must forget our local habits and attachments" and "be reduced to one faith and one government."[20] They saw in the new Constitution a government with authority extending "to every case that is of the least importance"[21] and capable of acting (preeminently in the crucial case of taxation) at discretion and independently of any agency but its own. Instead of thus destroying the federal character of the Union, "the leading feature of every amendment" of the Articles of Confederation ought to be, as Yates and Lansing expressed it, "the preservation of the individual states, in their uncontrouled constitutional rights, and . . . in reserving these, a mode might have been devised of granting to the confederacy, the monies arising from a general system of revenue; the power of regulating commerce, and enforcing the observance of foreign treaties, and other necessary matters of less moment."[22]

A few of the Anti-Federalists were not sure, it is true, that consolidation would be so bad, if it were really feasible. James Monroe went so far as to say that "to collect the citizens of America, who have fought and bled together, by whose joint and common efforts they have been raised to the comparatively happy and exalted theatre on which they now stand; to lay aside all those jarring interests and discordant principles, which state legislatures if they do not create, certainly foment and increase, arrange them under one government and make them one people, is an idea not only elevated and sublime, but equally benevolent and humane."[23] And, on the other hand, most of the Federalists agreed or professed to agree that consolidation was undesirable. Fisher Ames, defending the Constitution in Massachusetts, spoke the language of many Federalists when he insisted that "too much provision cannot be made against a consolidation. The state governments represent the wishes, and feelings, and local interests of the people. They are the safeguard and ornament of the Constitution; they will protract the period of our liberties; they will afford a shelter against the abuse of power, and will be the natural avengers of our violated rights."*[24] Indeed, expressions of rather strict federal principles were not uncommon on the Federalist side, although they were often perfunctory or shallow.

Perhaps the most conciliatory Federalist defense of federalism, and not accidentally one of the least satisfactory in principle, was contained in a line of argument put forward by James Wilson and some others to the effect that, just as individuals have to give up some of their natural rights to civil government to secure peaceful enjoyment of civil rights, so states must give up some of theirs to federal government in order to secure peaceful enjoyment of federal liberties.[25] But the analogy of civil liberty and federal liberty concedes the basic Anti-Federal contentions, and Wilson did not consistently adhere to it.[26] As each individual has one vote in civil society, for example, so each state ought, on this analogy, to have one vote in federal society. As the preservation of the rights of individuals is the object of civil society, so the preservation of the rights of states (not individuals) ought to be the object of federal society.[27] But these are Anti-Federal conclusions. Thus, when Agrippa assessed the proposed Constitution from the point of view of the interests of Massachusetts, he did so on *principled* ground, the same ground that properly leads any man to consider the civil society of which he is or may become a member, not exclusively but first and last, from the point of view of his interest in his life, liberty, and property.[28] Wilson, on the other hand, argued for the priority of the general interest of the Union over the particular interests of the states. And this position is not defensible—as Wilson's own argument sufficiently demonstrates—on the basis of the federal liberty–civil liberty analogy.*[29]

The more characteristic Federalist position was to deny that the choice lay between confederation and consolidation and to contend that in fact the Constitution provided a new form, partly national and partly federal. This was Publius' argument in *The Federalist,* no. 39. It was Madison's argument in the Virginia ratifying convention. And it was the usual argument of James Wilson himself, who emphasized the strictly limited powers of the general government and the essential part to be played in it by the states.[30] The Anti-Federalists objected that all such arguments foundered on the impossibility of dual sovereignty. "It is a solecism in politics for two co-ordinate sovereignties to exist together. . . ." A mixture may exist for a time, but it will inevitably tend in one direction or the other, subjecting the country in the meantime to "all the horrors of a divided sovereignty."[31] Luther Martin agreed with Madison that the new Constitution presented a novel mixture of federal and national elements; but he found it "just so much federal in appearance as to give its advocates in some measure, an opportunity of passing it as such upon the unsuspecting multitude, before they had time and opportunity to examine it, and yet so predominantly national as to put it in the power of its movers, whenever the machine shall be set agoing, to strike out every part that has the appearance of being federal, and to render it wholly and entirely a national government."[32]

The first words of the preamble sufficiently declare the anti-federal (in the strict sense) character of the Constitution, Patrick Henry thought; and his objection thundered over the Virginia convention sitting in Richmond:

[W]hat right had they to say, *We, the People*? My political curiosity, exclusive of my anxious solicitude for the public welfare, leads me to ask, who authorised them to speak the language of, *We, the People,* instead of *We, the States*? States are the characteristics, and the soul of a confederation. If the States be not the agents of this compact, it must be one great consolidated National Government of the people of all the States.[33]

The clearest minds among the Federalists agreed that states are the soul of a confederacy. That is what is wrong with confederacies: "The fundamental principle of the old Confederation is defective; we must totally eradicate and discard this principle before we can expect an efficient government."*[34]

Here lies the main significance of the mode of ratification in the proposed Constitution. The new procedure—ratification by special state conventions rather than by Congress and the state legislatures and provision that the

Constitution shall be established on ratification of nine states (as between them), rather than all thirteen states as required under the Articles of Confederation—was not merely illegal; it struck at the heart of the old Confederation. It denied, as Federalists like Hamilton openly admitted, the very basis of legality under the Articles of Confederation. The requirement in the Articles of Confederation for unanimous consent of the states to constitutional changes rested on the assumption that the states are the basic political entities, permanently associated indeed, but associated entirely at the will and in the interest of each of the several states.*[35] Even if it were granted that government under the Articles had collapsed (which most Anti-Federalists did not grant), there was no justification for abandoning the principles of state equality and unanimous consent to fundamental constitutional change. As William Paterson had put it in the Philadelphia Convention,

> If we argue the matter on the supposition that no Confederacy at present exists, it cannot be denied that all the States stand on the footing of equal sovereignty. All therefore must concur before any can be bound . . . If we argue on the fact that a federal compact actually exists, and consult the articles of it we still find an equal Sovereignty to be the basis of it.[36]

Whether in the Articles of Confederation or outside, the essential principle of American union was the equality of the states. As Luther Martin had argued in Philadelphia, "the separation from G. B. placed the 13 States in a state of nature towards each other; [and] they would have remained in that state till this time, but for the confederation. . . ."[37]

The provision for ratifying the Constitution rested, in the main, on the contrary assumption that the American states are not several political wholes, associated together according to their several wills and for the sake of their several interests, but are, and always were from the moment of their separation from the King of England, parts of one whole. Thus constitutional change is the business of the people, not of the state legislatures, though the people act in (or through) their states.*[38] As one nation divided into several states, moreover, constitutional change is to be decided, not by unanimous consent of separate and equal entities, but by the major part of a single whole—an extraordinary majority because of the importance of the question.*[39] The Federalists contended that the colonies declared their independence not individually but unitedly, and that they had never been independent of one another.*[40] And the implication of this view is that the foundation of government in the United States is the interest of the nation and not the interests of the states. "The Union is essential to our being as a nation. The pillars that prop it are crumbling to powder," said Fisher Ames, staggering through a metaphorical forest. "The Union is the vital sap that nourishes the tree."[41] The Articles of Confederation, in this view, were a defective instrument of a preexisting union.*[42] The congressional resolution calling for the Philadelphia Convention had described a means—"for the

13

sole and express purpose of revising the Articles of Confederation"—and an end—to "render the federal constitution adequate to the exigencies of Government & the preservation of the Union."[43] If there was any conflict, the means ought to be sacrificed to the end. The duty of the Philadelphia Convention and the members of the ratifying conventions was to take their bearings, not from the defective means, but from the great end, the preservation and well-being of the Union.*[44]

This view of the matter takes the debate beyond a consideration of legality or status quo, because the Federalists argued that what appeared to be legally or traditionally right was wrong when viewed in the light of the end of that law or tradition. The result was to force the Anti-Federalists, as it forced the opponents of strong national government in the Philadelphia Convention, to higher ground. It became necessary to consider the questions, what are the ends of the government of the Union, what are the ends of the governments of the states, and what is the proper relation between these ends and therefore between these governments?

3
The Small Republic

The Anti-Federalists' defense of federalism and of the primacy of the states rested on their belief that there was an inherent connection between the states and the preservation of individual liberty, which is the end of any legitimate government. Robert Whitehill of Pennsylvania, for example, feared that the proposed Constitution would be "the means of annihilating the constitutions of the several States, and consequently the liberties of the people. . . ."[1] "We are come hither," Patrick Henry urged his fellow Virginians, "to preserve the poor Commonwealth of Virginia, if it can be possibly done; Something must be done to preserve your liberty and mine."[2] The states have to be preserved because they are the natural homes of individual liberty. As Luther Martin had argued in Philadelphia:

At the separation from the British Empire, the people of America preferred the Establishment of themselves into thirteen separate sovereignties instead of incorporating themselves into one: to these they look up for the security of their lives, liberties, & properties: to these they must look up—The federal Govt. they formed, to defend the whole agst. foreign nations, in case of war, and to defend the lesser States agst. the ambition of the larger. . . .[3]

The governments instituted to secure the rights spoken of by the Declaration of Independence are the state governments. They do the primary business that governments are supposed to do. The government of the Union supplements the state governments, especially by giving them an external strength that none of them could manage on its own. But in principle the general government is subordinate to the state governments.

Why must the essential business of government be done by governmental units like the states? Primarily this was, in the Anti-Federalist view, a question of size. It was thought to have been demonstrated, historically and theoretically, that free, republican governments could extend only over a relatively small territory with a homogeneous population.*[4] Even among the states this rule was evident, for "the largest States are the Worst Governed."[5] One problem is that in large, diverse states many significant differences in condition, interest, and habit have to be ignored for the sake of uniform administration. Yet no genuine equality of government is possible in such a large state. The capital city, to take the prime example, will be close to some parts of the large state, but it will be remote, in every relevant sense, from the extremities.[6] A national government would be compelled to impose a crude uniform rule on American diversity, which would in fact result in hardship and inequity for many parts of the country.

Behind the administrative defects of a large republic lie three fundamental considerations, bearing on the kind of government needed in a free society. Only a small republic can enjoy a voluntary attachment of the people to the government and a voluntary obedience to the laws. Only a small republic can secure a genuine responsibility of the government to the people. Only a small republic can form the kind of citizens who will maintain republican government. These claims are central to the Anti-Federalist position.*[7]

It should be noted at the outset that there is a complication in the practical conclusions drawn from these considerations. Assuming the soundness of the case for the small republic and assuming that nothing but republican government is to be seriously considered for the United States, the obvious conclusion is that no attempt should be made to extend a single republican government over the whole United States. But if one republican government over the whole United States should nevertheless be unavoidable, despite serious disadvantages, then the Anti-Federalist arguments for the small republic serve the practical purpose of revealing and helping to minimize these disadvantages. Cognizance of the advantages of the small republic may be helpful in avoiding the worst disadvantages of a large one. In the discussion that follows we shall be meeting both kinds of arguments. Some defend the idea of the small republic simply; others (drawn from the same theoretical source) aim to improve or mitigate the dangers of the large republic that American circumstances seemed to require. The different kinds of arguments will be clear enough as we go along, but both the distinction and the common source should be kept in mind.

The dependence of any republican government on the confidence of the people was one of the reasons given by the nationalists in the Constitutional Convention, notably James Wilson, for resting the general government directly on the people. Wilson "was for raising the federal pyramid to a considerable altitude, and for that reason wished to give it as broad a basis as possible. No government could long subsist without the confidence of the people. In a republican Government this confidence was peculiarly essential."[8] The Anti-Federalists emphatically endorsed this principle. "The great object of a free people," The Federal Farmer argued, "must be so to form their government and laws, and so to administer them, as to create a confidence in, and respect for the laws; and thereby induce the sensible and virtuous part of the community to declare in favor of the laws, and to support them without an expensive military force."*[9] But the Anti-Federalists denied that the simple expedient of having the people elect federal representatives was enough to secure their attachment. In a large republic the people "will have no confidence in their legislature, suspect them of ambitious views, be jealous of every measure they adopt, and will not support the laws they pass."[10] Both reason and experience prove,

Richard Henry Lee wrote, that so extensive and various a territory as the United States "cannot be governed in freedom" except in a confederation of states. Within each state, "opinion founded on the knowledge of those who govern, procures obedience without force. But remove the opinion, which must fall with a knowledge of characters in so widely extended a country, and force then becomes necessary to secure the purposes of civil government. . . ." The general rule is that government must exist, if not by persuasion, then by force.*[11] In a large empire standing armies are necessary "to cure the defect of the laws" and to take the place of popular confidence in and respect for the government.*[12]

The second characteristic of the small republic is its capacity to ensure a strict responsibility of the government to the people. In a direct democracy, responsibility is ensured by the absence of much differentiation between the people and their government. However, most of the Anti-Federalists admitted the need, under American conditions at least, for a system of representation as a substitute for the meeting together of all the citizens.[13] The problem, then, was to keep the representatives responsible, in the rather narrow meaning of that term, that is, directly answerable to and dependent on their constituents.[14] This is the reason for the concern with short terms of office, frequent rotation, and a numerous representation.[15] The Anti-Federalists understood, however, that such devices are insufficient. Effective and thoroughgoing responsibility is to be found only in a likeness between the representative body and the citizens at large. Thus "a full and equal representation is that which possesses the same interests, feelings, opinions, and views the people themselves would were they all assembled. . . ." According to Melancton Smith, representatives "should be a true picture of the people; possess the knowledge of their circumstances and their wants; sympathize in all their distresses, and be disposed to seek their true interests."[16] This describes the state legislatures reasonably well, it was claimed, but the federal legislature could not even come close to being representative in this genuine sense, at least not without a sharp increase in its number. Federal elections will present the voters with a choice among representatives of the well-known few, or the "natural aristocracy" as the Anti-Federalists often called them.*[17] "It is deceiving a people to tell them they are electors, and can chuse their legislators, if they cannot, in the nature of things, chuse men from among themselves, and genuinely like themselves."[18]

What is wanted in a representative system is not "brilliant talents" but "a sameness, as to residence and interests, between the representative and his constituents." No great talents are necessary for government, and the men of great abilities are, on the whole, a danger rather than a benefit to a republic.*[19] If, however, the Anti-Federalists distrusted "great abilities," they were willing to admit that "sameness" in a representative body is not literally possible. Every representative body is more aristocratic than the

17

body of the people by whom it is chosen,[20] and any representative body covering the whole United States would inevitably be highly selective. Here the argument shifts from the desirability of the small republic to the mitigation of the evils of the large one.*[21] Given the need, especially in the general government, for some considerable compromise of the principle of sameness, the Anti-Federalists' secondary, more practical goal was a representation large enough to secure a substantial (if not proportionate) representation of the middling classes, in particular the sturdy yeomanry. This view was based not on a presumption of intrinsic superiority in the yeoman but on the political consequences of his peculiar situation. Melancton Smith gave the Anti-Federalist argument in his classic confrontation with Alexander Hamilton on the subject of representation.

The same passions and prejudices govern all men. The circumstances in which men are placed in a great measure give a cast to the human character. Those in middling circumstances, have less temptation—they are inclined by habit and the company with whom they associate, to set bounds to their passions and appetites—if this is not sufficient, the want of means to gratify them will be a restraint—they are obliged to employ their time in their respective callings—hence the substantial yeomanry of the country are more temperate, of better morals, and less ambitious than the great. . . .When . . . this class in society pursue their own interest, they promote that of the public, for it is involved in it.[22]

All are agreed, Sydney argued, "that the rights and liberties of a country were ever in danger from the rich and poor, and their safety in the middle sort or yeomanry of the country. . . ."[23] An adequate representation of the middling classes serves, then, as a practical and effective substitute for a full representation of the people; for it does not require an excessively large body, and yet in pursuing their own interests the middling classes tend to pursue the interests of the public at large. However, the proposed House of Representatives failed not only the strict test of sameness but the looser test of adequate representation of the middling classes. Given the number of representatives and the proportion of representatives and people, few if any of the members of this class could expect to be elected.*[24] The Anti-Federalists generally saw this as an inherent deficiency of any nationwide government, yet, as we shall see, they accepted the need for such a government. If this was a contradiction it was not, they thought, due to any deficiency in their reasoning, for it lay at the heart of the American situation. The prudent course was to confine the contradiction to the narrowest possible scope by, on the one hand, making the representation in the first branch of the national legislature as full as circumstances permitted and, on the other hand, leaving as much of the power as possible in the states, where genuine responsibility could exist.

A related aspect of the question of responsibility concerned the much-discussed issue of jury trial, which it was alleged the Constitution would weaken or destroy. There is no need here to go into detail, but the crux of the objection lay in the political significance of the jury trial. While an adequate representation in at least one branch of the legislature was indispensable at the top, law-making, level, the jury trial provided the people's safeguard at the bottom, administrative, level. "Juries are constantly and frequently drawn from the body of the people, and freemen of the country; and by holding the jury's right to return a general verdict in all cases sacred, we secure to the people at large, their just and rightful controul in the judicial department."*25 A [Maryland] Farmer argued, indeed, that the jury trial is more important than representation in the legislature, because "those usurpations, which silently undermine the spirit of liberty, under the sanction of law, are more dangerous than direct and open legislative attacks. . . ."26 The main point, however, is that the democratic branch of the legislature and the jury trial are the means of effective and lawful popular control. They "are the means by which the people are let into the knowledge of public affairs—are enabled to stand as the guardians of each others rights, and to restrain, by regular and legal measures, those who otherwise might infringe upon them." The often extreme and apparently unfounded claims by the Anti-Federalists that the proposed Constitution would destroy the trial by jury should be seen against this background. The question was not fundamentally whether the lack of adequate provision for jury trial would weaken a traditional bulwark of individual rights (although that was also involved) but whether it would fatally weaken the role of the people in the *administration* of government.*27

The third part of the Anti-Federalist defense of the small republic concerned the kind of citizens a free republic needs. The Anti-Federalists emphasized repeatedly that the character of a people is affected by government and laws, but that that relation had been dangerously ignored in the framing of the proposed Constitution. In the words of Melancton Smith, "Government operates upon the spirit of the people, as well as the spirit of the people operates upon it—and if they are not conformable to each other, the one or the other will prevail. . . . Our duty is to frame a government friendly to liberty and the rights of mankind, which will tend to cherish and cultivate a love of liberty among our citizens." "If there are advantages," The Federal Farmer argued, "in the equal division of our lands, and the strong and manly habits of our people, we ought to establish governments calculated to give duration to them, and not governments which never can work naturally, till that equality of property, and those free and manly habits shall be destroyed; these evidently are not the natural basis of the proposed constitution."*28

A republican citizenry must be free and independent-minded, but it must also be homogeneous. "In a republic, the manners, sentiments, and interests of the people should be similar. If this be not the case, there will be a constant clashing of opinions; and the representatives of one part will be continually striving against those of the other. This will retard the operations of government, and prevent such conclusions as will promote the public good." Only within the relatively small communities formed by the individual states could such homogeneity be found. Given the variety of climates, productions, laws, and customs among the United States, a legislature formed of representatives from all parts of the country "would be composed of such heterogeneous and discordant principles, as would constantly be contending with each other."[29] The preservation of homogeneity required, for many of the Anti-Federalists, protection against foreign contamination. "To what purpose have you expended so freely the blood and treasures of this country? To have a government with unlimited powers administered by foreigners?"[30] Arguing that the general government should not be given the power to naturalize aliens, Agrippa pointed to the contrasting results of Pennsylvania's policy of open immigration and the eastern states' freedom from foreign mixture. Whereas Pennsylvania purchased her size and population at the expense of religion and good morals, "the eastern states have, by keeping separate from the foreign mixtures, acquired their present greatness in the course of a century and a half, and have preserved their religion and morals." At the same time they have preserved "that manly virtue which is equally fitted for rendering them respectable in war, and industrious in peace."[31]

Homogeneity implied, for the Anti-Federalists, not only likeness but likeness of a certain kind: a society in which there are no extremes of wealth, influence, education, or anything else—the homogeneity of a moderate, simple, sturdy, and virtuous people.[32] Republican government depends on civic virtue, on a devotion to fellow citizens and to country so deeply instilled as to be almost as automatic and powerful as the natural devotion to self-interest. Many Anti-Federalists joined Patrick Henry in praise of the Swiss, who "have retained their independence, republican simplicity and valour."[33] These qualities are encouraged in the restricted sphere of the small republic, which offers little inducement or opportunity for the exercise of divisive and corrupting talents and which daily reminds each man of the benefits derived from and the duties owed to his little community.

Wherever they looked in the new Constitution the Anti-Federalists saw threats to civic virtue. The federal city provided for would breed monarchical institutions and courtly habits, with their oppressive tendencies and with the effect "above all [of] the perpetual ridicule of virtue."[34] The standing army would be not only a potential instrument of oppression but a source of moral corruption. With interests and habits different from the rest of the community, a standing army "will inevitably sow the seeds of corruption and depravity of manners. Indolence will increase, and with it crimes cannot but increase. The springs of honesty will gradually grow lax, and chaste and severe manners be succeeded by those that are dissolute and vicious. When a standing army is kept up, virtue never thrives."[35] Commerce itself, the benefits of which were one of the major reasons for the American Union, seemed to threaten republican simplicity and virtue.[36] Commerce is the vehicle of distinctions in wealth, of foreign influence, and of the decline of morals. "As people become more luxurious, they become more incapacitated of governing themselves."[37] Anti-Federalists constantly complained of America's hankering after European luxury. They agreed generally with John Adams that "frugality is a great revenue, besides curing us of vanities, levities, and fopperies, which are real antidotes to all great, manly, and warlike virtues."[38]

Implicit in all of these opinions relating to republican citizenship is a concern with civic education, broadly conceived. Mercy Warren, who saw as deeply into this question as any of her contemporaries, flirted with the isolationism that tempted many of the Anti-Federalists. Could the pure republican spirit of the Americans be preserved, she reflected, by walling the country off from European luxury, on the one hand, and western empire on the other? It could not. However high the walls of separation, the fingers of avarice and ambition would find their ways through or around them. The danger to the republican spirit of America was illustrated by American attraction to European luxury and skepticism; but the source of the danger was not external. It lay, as it always lies, in the restless ambition and avarice in the heart of every man and every people; and that is where it must be met, principally by education. "[I]f the education of youth, both public and private, is attended to, their industrious and economical habits maintained, their moral character and that assemblage of virtues supported, which is necessary for the happiness of individuals and of nations, there is not much danger that they will for a long time be subjugated by the arms of foreigners, or that their republican system will be subverted by the arts of domestic enemies."[39] A few Anti-Federalists made specific proposals. Thus A [Maryland] Farmer proposed the establishment of local "seminaries of useful learning, with professorships of political and domestic œconomy." The citizens should be instructed not in "the philosophy of the moon and skies," but in "what is useful in this world—the principles of free government, illustrated by the history of mankind—the sciences of morality, agriculture, commerce, the management of farms and household affairs." If this were done in a short time "the people instead of abusing, would wade up to their knees in blood, to defend their governments."[40] More often the Anti-Federalist thought of the whole organization of the polity as having an educative function. The small republic was seen as a school of citizenship as much as a scheme for government. An important part—much more important than we are today likely to remember—of their argument for a federal bill of rights was the educative function of such a document in reminding the citizen of the ends of civil government and in strengthening his attachment to it. The provisions of a bill of rights "can inspire and conserve the affection for the native country, they will be the first lesson of the young citizens becoming men, to sustain the dignity of their being. . . ."[41]

Finally, many Anti-Federalists were concerned with the maintenance of religious conviction as a support of republican government. "Refiners may weave as fine a web of reason as they please, but the experience of all times," Richard Henry Lee wrote to James Madison in 1784, "shews Religion to be the guardian of morals."[42] The opinions of men need to be formed "in favour of virtue and religion. . . ."[43] Religious support of political institutions is an old idea, and here again the Anti-Federalists tended to be the conservatives. The view was well expressed by an anonymous Massachusetts writer in 1787.[44] He explained that there are but three ways of controlling the "turbulent passions of mankind": by punishment; by reward; and "by prepossessing the people in favour of virtue by affording publick protection to religion." All are necessary, but especially the last. "[I]t is not more difficult to build an elegant house without tools to work with, than it is to establish a durable government without the public protection of religion." By 1787, however, the opinion seemed to be growing that organized religion could be dispensed with or taken for granted. This was, at any rate, the Anti-Federal reading of the situation. The indifference of the Constitution and its main defenders to organized religion was striking. In the words of Federalist writer Elihu, "the light of philosophy has arisen," and "mankind are no longer to be deluded with fable." "Making the glory of God subservient to the temporal interest of men, is a worn-out trick. . . ."[45] Anti-Federalists saw quite clearly the implications of such arguments and challenged them. They would have agreed with an anonymous Virginian who urged that steps be taken to revitalize religion: "Whatever influence speculative vanity may ascribe to the indefinite principle termed honor, or political refinement, to an artful collusion of interest, sound reason as well as experience proves that a due sense of responsibility to the Deity, as the author of those moral laws, an observance of which constitutes the happiness and welfare of societies as well as individuals, is the mean most likely to give a right direction to the conduct of mankind."[46] The Anti-Federalists feared that the Americans would follow the example of the Europeans as described by Mercy Warren: "Bent on gratification, at the expense of every moral tie, they have broken down the barriers of religion, and the spirit of infidelity is nourished at the fount; thence the poisonous streams run through every grade that constitutes the mass of nations." Warren insisted that skepticism is not, as some hold, necessarily fostered by republican liberty. Indeed, the history of republics is the history of strict regard to religion.[47]

It is less easy to say what concrete form the Anti-Federalists thought this concern with religion ought to take. They favored religious toleration and sometimes criticized the Constitution for the absence of protection of liberty of conscience; but this was assumed to mean, in practice, toleration of Christian (or only Protestant) sects and was rarely extended even in principle to the protection of professed atheists. They saw no inconsistency between liberty of conscience and the public support of the religious, and generally Protestant, community as the basis of public and private morality. Many Anti-Federalists supported and would even have strengthened the mild religious establishments that existed in some states. Richard Henry Lee wrote in 1784 that "he must be a very inattentive observer in our Country, who does not see that avarice is accomplishing the destruction of religion, for want of a legal obligation to contribute something to its support. The [Virginia] declaration of Rights, it seems to me, rather contends against forcing modes of faith and forms of worship, than against compelling contribution for the support of religion in general."*48 More generally, the Anti-Federalist position was not so much that government ought to foster religion as that the consolidating Constitution threatened the healthy religious situation as it then existed. The religious diversity of the whole United States seemed so great as to strain to breaking point any publicly useful religious foundation for the nation as a whole. Consolidation would require, then, substituting for religion some other foundation of political morality—which the Anti-Federalists foresaw would be an aggregate of selfish interests held together by force. This tendency would be strengthened by the absence from the Constitution of any religious test for officeholding, which seemed intended to further undermine the public significance of religious conviction.*49 The Constitution and its defenders deliberately turned away from religion as the foundation of civil institutions. Among the Anti-Federalists, on the other hand, there was a great deal of sympathy with views like those of Charles Turner: "without the prevalance of *Christian piety and morals,* the best republican Constitution can never save us from slavery and ruin." Turner hoped that the first Congress under the Constitution would recommend to the states the institution of such means of education "as shall be *adequate* to the *divine, patriotick purpose* of training up the children and youth at large, in that solid learning, and in those pious and moral principles, which are the *support,* the *life* and SOUL of republican government and liberty, of which a free Constitution is the body. . . ." He expressed a central Anti-Federal thought when he urged that the new rulers should turn their attention to the task, which surpasses the framing of constitutions, of fostering religion and morals, thereby making government less necessary by rendering "the people more capable of being *a Law to themselves.*"50 Such self-government was possible, however, only if the center of gravity of American government remained in the states.

4

Union

While the Anti-Federalists were concerned with individual liberty, which they thought depended on republican virtue, which in turn depended on maintaining the primacy of the states, they also wanted Union, to provide defense against foreign enemies, to promote and protect American commerce, and to maintain order among the states. "The first thing I have at heart is American *liberty*," Patrick Henry said; "the second thing is American Union. . . ." Melancton Smith "was as strongly impressed with the necessity of a Union, as any one could be: He would seek it with as much ardor." He was ready "to sacrifice every thing for a Union, except the liberties of his country, than which he could contemplate no greater misfortune." He hoped we were not reduced to the dreadful alternative of choosing one or the other.[1] The Anti-Federalists, like their opponents, spoke of the American "nation" or "country." They emphatically resisted the suggestion, which the Federalists tried to plant (with some but not much basis), that they were favorably disposed toward a breakup of the Union into separate confederacies.[*2] Everyone agreed, Merrill Jensen has written, that the United States was a nation; "they disagreed as to whether the new nation should have a federal or a national government."[*3] This is accurate enough so long as it is recognized that a debate over whether a nation should have a national government amounts to a debate over whether it shall *be* a nation. That at least is what the Federalists claimed, and the Anti-Federalists could scarcely deny it.[*4]

Generally the Anti-Federalists admitted that a more efficient federal government was needed, although they qualified this admission in a variety of ways. Some insisted that the true bond of union was a sense of mutual interest and mutual obligation, not governmental strength. The most elaborate version of this argument was presented by Agrippa, who rejected a consolidated American empire on the characteristic Anti-Federal grounds that we have already examined. A Union based on political power would result in debasement of the people and insecurity of rights. Must the states, then, separate?

This would be true if there was no principle to substitute in the room of power. Fortunately there is one. This is commerce. All the states have local advantages, and in a considerable degree separate interests. They are, therefore, in a situation to supply each other's wants. Carolina, for instance, is inhabited by planters, while the Massachusetts is more engaged in commerce and manufactures. Congress has the power of deciding their differences. The most friendly intercourse may therefore be established between them. A diversity of produce, wants and interests, produces commerce, and commerce, where there is a common, equal and moderate authority to preside, produces friendship.[5]

The same principle applies to the new settlers in the west. "Here then we have a bond of union which applies to all parts of the empire, and would continue to operate if the empire comprehended all America." The bond of Union is to be found not in political power but in a system of diverse but harmonious economic interests. Difficulty creeps in, however, when Agrippa admits the need for "a common, equal and moderate authority to preside" over the commercial intercourse. Congress must have the power to decide differences among the states. Thus it would appear that political power is, after all, a necessary condition of the bond of Union. Even granting this, however—and it can hardly be denied—Agrippa's formulation emphasizes the *facilitating* character of federal political power, in contrast to the governing power that seemed to be provided in the Constitution. The function of the presiding political authority ought to be merely to serve commercial intercourse among the states. On this basis Agrippa could suggest very limited augmentations of the power of the general government, augmentations kept from undue expansion by a clear view of the true bond of American Union, which is commercial intercourse based on mutual needs.*[6]

The basic difficulty with this argument is that it relies decisively on the voluntary recognition of mutual dependence. The Anti-Federalists were inclined to hope, with James Monroe, that, once a substantial (but still very limited) national government was established, "their constitutional demands, or requisitions, would be complied with."[7] But the futility of this hope was the greatest lesson of the history of the Articles of Confederation. It was precisely what had led the country into what Publius described as "the last stage of national humiliation." Engagements broken, debts unpaid, credit dried up, commerce stagnated, territory violated, remonstrances scorned—in short, Publius asked, "what indication is there of national disorder, poverty and insignificance that could befal a community so peculiarly blessed with natural advantages as we are, which does not form a part of the dark catalogue of our public misfortunes?"[8]

The Anti-Federalists tried to soften the stark outlines of the many pictures of this kind painted by the advocates of the Constitution. They tried to show that the circumstances of the United States were not so bad as they were described and that such evils as did exist were less the result of defects in the Articles of Confederation than of peculiar economic and political circumstances. Moreover, they alleged that the existing government had been deliberately weakened by Federalist criticism exaggerating both the urgency and the extent of the difficulties. In any case there was no reason to abandon ordinary prudence. "Is it probable, that we shall ever be in a situation, in which we can with more temper and greater safety, deliberate upon this momentous concern than at present?"*9

Yet while the Anti-Federalists objected to exaggerations of American troubles, at least equally striking is the extent to which they accepted the broad outlines of the picture painted by the friends of the Constitution. It is difficult to see how Forrest McDonald can describe Philadelphians in 1787 as "serenely unaware that historians were one day to know this as the Critical Period of American history. . . ."[10] Even if the Anti-Federalists had uniformly asserted that the country was prosperous and untroubled, they could hardly have been unaware of the persistent Federalist arguments to the contrary, in which the very phrase, "critical period," figured prominently.*[11] But in fact the Anti-Federalists were less sanguine about the conditions of the country and the capacity of government under the Articles than some of their later apologists have been. The description of An Old Whig is not typical, but it is by no means unique: "we are not suffered to be the carriers of our own produce. . . . Our shipwrights are starved, our seamen driven abroad for want of employ, our timber left useless on our hands, our ironworks . . . now almost reduced to nothing, and our money banished from the country." These circumstances, following a loss of trade, "have justly alarmed us all. . . ."[12] "I know our situation is critical," wrote the most prominent and one of the most moderate of the Anti-Federalist pamphleteers, "and it behooves us to make the best of it."[13] If the alternative really had been to admit the proposed Constitution or "be left to our present weakness, confusion and distress," many Anti-Federalists would have agreed with An Old Whig and voted for the Constitution.[14] Few Anti-Federalists would in fact have objected to the designation of 1787 as the "critical period," and many used that or synonymous phrases.*[15]

The Anti-Federalists did tend to argue that the difficulties experienced by the country were not mainly caused by an ineffective general government. Not stronger government but time and industry were needed to rectify the distresses following the war.[16] A distinction should be made, insisted Candidus, between the difficulties arising from the government and those arising from our own imprudence or unfavorable circumstances; and when this is done it will be seen that only modest governmental reform is necessary.[17] The true cause of American difficulties lay deeper than forms of government. "Unhappily for us, immediately after our extrication from a cruel and unnatural war, luxury and dissipation overran the country, banishing all that economy, frugality, and industry, which had been exhibited during the war."[18] As Richard Henry Lee wrote in the spring of 1787, "I fear it is more in vicious manners, than mistakes in form, that we must seek for the causes of the present discontent."[19] The analysis of Candidus is important and characteristic enough to quote at some length.

Upon the whole, we are too apt to charge those misfortunates to the want of energy in our government, which we have brought upon ourselves by dissipation and extravagance; and we are led to flatter ourselves, that the proposed Constitution will restore to us peace and happiness, notwithstanding we should neglect to acquire these blessings by industry and frugality.—I will venture to affirm, that the extravagance of our British importations,—the discouragement of our own manufactures, and the luxurious living of all ranks and degrees, have been the principal cause of all the evils we now experience; and a general reform in these particulars, would have a greater tendency to promote the welfare of these States, than any measures that could be adopted.—No government under heaven could have preserved a people from ruin, or kept their commerce from declining, when they were exhausting their valuable resources in paying for superfluities, and running themselves in debt to *foreigners,* and to *each other* for articles of folly and dissipation:—While this is the case, we may contend about forms of government, but no establishment will enrich a people, who wantonly spend beyond their income.[20]

Some governmental improvements may be desirable, but those who look to a new government for the solution of American difficulties look in the wrong place and at the same time tend to increase the real difficulties.

May not *our manners* be the source of our national evils? May not our attachment to foreign trade increase them? Have we not acted imprudently in exporting almost all our gold and silver for foreign luxuries? It is now acknowledged that we have not a sufficient quantity of the precious metals to answer the various purposes of government and commerce; and without a breach of charity, it may be said that this deficiency arises from the want of public virtue, in prefering private interest to every other consideration.[21]

If, however, the country's domestic and economic problems were both less serious and less amenable to constitutional remedy than the Federalists contended, what of the obvious weakness of the United States under the Articles of Confederation in dealing with other nations? The Anti-Federalists agreed with Publius that "if we are to be one nation in any respect, it clearly ought to be in respect to other nations."[22] They were likely to emphasize, however, America's isolated situation and the unlikelihood of European powers involving themselves with the United States even to collect unpaid debts. Few Anti-Federalists went quite so far as Patrick Henry, but there was a good deal of hopeful sympathy with his view that as far as danger from European nations was concerned, "you may sleep in safety forever for them."[23] Wilson Nicholas characterized the Anti-Federalist argument, with much justice, as "turn[ing] upon [the] supposition: —*We shall always have peace, and need make no provision against wars.* Is not this deceiving ourselves? Is it not fallacious? Did there ever exist a nation which, at some period or other, was not exposed to war?"[24] The Anti-Federalists replied that if war does come, what will count will be not great armies and navies but the American spirit, that very manly independence and love of country that also supports American liberty. The kind of governmental strength promised by the Constitution is deceptive, for it tends to undermine the popular independence and virtue that are the true backbone of a republic. George Mason had made this argument in the Philadelphia convention, when he compared the strength of a unitary executive with the deeper strength of a virtuous republican citizenry, and it was often repeated in the debate over ratification.[25] "For a new country to become strong and energetic, so as to be able to repel a foreign foe, the government must be *free* and *patriotic,* and the people must be *wealthy* and *well-affected* to it." "[T]he people will never fight (if they can help it) for representation, taxes and rags."[26] The Federalists exaggerated the problem of national defense and proposed the wrong solution. If there was any danger, Henry affirmed, "I would recur to the American spirit to defend us."*[27]

In both the domestic and the foreign spheres, then, the Anti-Federalists thought that the Federalists overstated the American difficulties and the extent to which they could be corrected by constitutional reform. They thought that, as Federalist propaganda against the Articles of Confederation had helped to increase the difficulties, so Federalist propaganda in defense of the Constitution might divert attention from the true cause of trouble, the deterioration of the American spirit. Far from arresting this deterioration, the Constitution seemed likely to intensify it.

When all of these qualifications are made and all these doubts stated, however, the Anti-Federalists nevertheless agreed that a Union was wanted, that it required an efficient government, and that the Articles of Confederation did not provide such a government. "The importance of preserving an union, and of establishing a government equal to the purpose of maintaining that union, is a sentiment deeply impressed on the mind of every citizen of America. It is now no longer doubted, that the confederation, in its present form, is inadequate to that end: Some reform in our government must take place. In this all parties agree. . . ." "It is on all hands acknowledged that the federal government is not adequate to the purpose of the Union."[28]

An efficient federal government need not, however, imply one so powerful as that proposed in the Constitution. The broad grants of power, taken together with the "supremacy" and the "necessary and proper" clauses, amounted, the Anti-Federalists contended, to an unlimited grant of power to the general government to do whatever it might choose to do. In the provision (Art. I, sec. 4) granting Congress the power to alter state regulations, or make its own, regarding the times, places, and manner of electing senators and representatives, for example, the Anti-Federalists saw endless possibility of usurpation and tyranny.[29] Could any possible good compensate for the dangers of such a provision? Moreover, the Anti-Federalists insisted, in contradiction to their opponents, that the powers of the proposed government, not its organization, was the central question.[30] All of the arguments of the Federalists that this new government was better constructed than the old one fell before the massive fact that the old government was weak and this one would be strong. "The old Confederation is so defective in point of power," William Grayson plaintively explained to the Virginia convention, "that no danger can result from creating offices under it; because those who hold them cannot be paid. . . . Why not make this system as secure as that, in this respect?"[31] Not many Anti-Federalists were quite so transparent, but their opponents were quick to insist that Grayson's position was precisely the ridiculous conclusion to which the Anti-Federalist argument led: without the power to do good, a government can do no harm. But a government must have the capacity to accomplish its ends, otherwise liberty itself is in danger: "there is no way more likely to lose ones liberty in the end than being too niggardly of it in the beginning. . . ."[32] The means, the Federalists argued again and again, must be proportioned to the end, and the end in the case of the general government is not capable of being limited in advance. As bounds cannot be set to a nation's wants, so bounds ought not to be set to its resources. "The contingencies of society are not reducible to calcula tions. They cannot be fixed or bounded, even in imagination."

The framers of constitutions must see that "no power should be wanting which the safety of the community requires." Otherwise, when critical occasions arise, the country will suffer the alternative of usurpation or catastrophe. Of course every power can be abused, and abuse must be guarded against; but "our risk of this evil [is] one of the conditions of the imperfect state of human nature, where there is no good without the mixture of some evil."[33] Publius drove the point home:

For the absurdity must continually stare us in the face of confiding to a government the direction of the most essential national interests, without daring to trust it to the authorities which are indispensable to their proper and efficient management. Let us not attempt to reconcile contradictions, but firmly embrace a rational alternative.[34]

This is a powerful argument, given the Anti-Federalists' own desire for a Union government powerful enough to secure common interests, especially defense. It is an argument that is almost sufficient to justify the Constitution; and it was in fact the main argument of many of the Federalist leaders and writers. Many of the Anti-Federalists simply could not meet it; but others made a series of attempts to resist the apparently invincible logic of unlimited means to accomplish unlimitable ends. They contended that it is always prudent to grant power cautiously and that it is possible to make reasonable estimates of the limited means needed under ordinary circumstances. It is safer, especially in a republic, to be guided by such estimates than by remote and extreme possibilities. Moreover, they charged that the Federalists were more or less deliberately using an argument about means to enlarge the ends of government, shifting their gaze from individual liberty to visions of national empire and glory. Finally they tried to show that the state governments also have their ends, that these are in fact the primary ends of government, and that these also require appropriate means.

The prudence of granting power cautiously was a common Anti-Federal refrain. Governmental power should always be granted with a niggardly hand, a maxim that applies a hundredfold to this proposed general government, distant and dangerous as it must necessarily be even if improved. "As the poverty of individuals prevents luxury, so the poverty of publick bodies, whether sole or aggregate, prevents tyranny. A nation cannot, perhaps, do a more politick thing, than to supply the purse of its sovereign with that parsimony, which results from a sense of the labour it costs, and so to compel him to comply with the genius of his people, and conform to their situation, whether he will or not."[35] Again and again, Anti-Federalists argued in terms like those of a Massachusetts delegate who said that "we had a right to be jealous of our rulers, who ought never to have a power which they could abuse." Again and again Federalists answered in terms like those of Mr. Rutledge in South Carolina, that "the very idea of power included a possibility of doing harm; and if the gentleman would show the power that could do no harm, he would at once discover it to be a power that could do no good."[36] But to concede the Federalist point does not overcome the difficulty the Anti-Federalists raised. "There is no public *abuse*," A [Maryland] Farmer argued, "that does not spring from the necessary *use* of power,—it is that insensible progress from the *use* to the *abuse*, that has led mankind through scenes of calamity and woe, that makes us now shrink back with horror, from the history of our species."[37] Prudence dictates granting too few powers rather than too many; rulers will always exercise their full legal powers, and it is easier to increase power than to lessen it. Nor is it sufficient to say that the exigencies facing the general government are in principle illimitable. Reasonable estimates can in practice be made and acted upon: ". . . every nation may form a rational judgment, what force will be competent to protect and defend it, against any enemy with which it is probable it may have to contend."[38] It is far more prudent to act upon such judgments than to rush to provide the government at once with all the power it may conceivably need. The maxim that unlimited means are necessary to meet unlimited ends is balanced by the maxim, which applies to all forms of power, "that all governments find a use for as much money as they can raise."[39] Extraordinary needs can be met as they arise. If a national credit and a national treasury are needed in time of war, let them be provided in time of war, Patrick Henry said; republics always put forth their utmost resources when required.[40]

Indeed, the stress placed by Federalists on national defense and a vigorous commercial policy often seemed to mask a radical shift in direction from the protection of individual liberty to the pursuit of national riches and glory. When the Anti-Federalists saw the new Constitution defended as having the "noble purposes" to make us "respectable as a nation abroad, and rich as individuals at home" and as calculated to promote "the grandeur and importance of America, until time shall be no more,"[41] they feared for the principles of the American governments. "You are not to inquire how your trade may be increased," Patrick Henry warned, "nor how you are to become a great and powerful people, but how your liberties can be secured; for liberty ought to be the direct end of your Government."

Shall we imitate the example of those nations who have gone from a simple to a splendid Government? Are those nations more worthy of our imitation? What can make an adequate satisfaction to them for the loss they have suffered in attaining such a Government—for the loss of their liberty? If we admit this Consolidated Government, it will be because we like a great splendid one. Some way or other we must be a great and mighty empire; we must have an army, and a navy, and a number of things: When the American spirit was in its youth, the language of America was different: Liberty, Sir, was then the primary object.*[42]

Ambitious Federalists, captivated by visions of "stately palaces" and "dazzling ideas of glory, wealth, and power," wanted us *to be like other nations.*"[43] That is just what we should not be. Americans "ought to furnish the world with an example of a great people, who in their civil institutions hold chiefly in view, the attainment of virtue, and happiness among ourselves. Let the monarchs in Europe, share among them the glory of depopulating countries, and butchering thousands of their innocent citizens, to revenge private quarrels, or to punish an insult offered to a wife, a mistress, or a favorite: I envy them not the honor, and I pray heaven this country may never be ambitious of it."[44] The splendor of the monarch, and the power of the government are one thing," The Federal Farmer wrote. "The happiness of the subject depends on very different causes. . . ."[45] Wars might be necessary, but they should be strictly defensive. The Anti-Federalists generally held to what Hamilton scornfully called "the novel and absurd experiment in politics of tying up the hands of government from offensive war founded upon reasons of state";[46] and they saw in Hamilton's scorn dangerous dreams of national glory. "War is justifiable on no other principle than self-defence, it is at best a curse to any people; it is comprehensive of most, if not all the mischiefs that do or can afflict mankind; it depopulates nations; lays waste the finest countries; destroys arts and sciences, it many times ruins the best men, and advances the worst, it effaces every trace of virtue, piety and compassion, and introduces all kinds of corruption in public affairs; and in short, is pregnant with so many evils, that it ought ever to be avoided if possible; nothing but self-defense can justify it."[47]

The tendency of the Federalists to inflate national concerns was connected with their failure to recognize that defense and commercial advantage are not the only ends of government. The state governments also have their ends, and require adequate means to pursue them. Granting fully the indispensability of an effective general government, it is still the states to which is entrusted the "most important end of government," the direction of the internal police and economy; and the happiness of the people depends "infinitely more on this than it does upon all that glory and respect which nations achieve by the most brilliant martial achievements. . . ." The just way of reasoning on this subject, then, is that the general government ought to have the authority to discharge its responsibilities for defense, foreign relations, and general commerce, "so far as is consistent with the providing for our internal protection and defence" by the state governments.[48] The American federal system is seen here as containing parallel governments in a kind of balance or tension with one another.

Neither the general government, nor the state governments, ought to be vested with all the powers proper to be exercised for promoting the ends of government. The powers are divided between them—certain ends to be attained by the one, and other certain ends by the other; and these, taken together, include all the ends of good government. This being the case, the conclusion follows, that each should be furnished with the means, to attain the ends, to which they are designed.[49]

The claims of one side must not be pressed so far as to incapacitate the other. In particular, the more urgent and more obvious claims of the general government must not be allowed to override the more fundamental claims of the states.

We come at this point in the discussion to a shift, which occurred gradually and erratically during the ratification debate, in the meaning of the term "federal" and the understanding of the American "federal" system. The early or relatively "pure" Anti-Federal position, as we have shown, was a defense of federalism in a rather strict sense, understood as the principle of a league or confederation, as we now call it.[50] The Federalist counter was to show that a merely federal government could not perform the tasks that even the Anti-Federalists would give to a general government, that the Articles of Confederation themselves were not purely federal, and that the proposed government under the Constitution was neither simply national nor simply federal but a combination of them. The mixture permeates all aspects of the constitutional system—or so, at least it was claimed—but for the present what is crucial is the constitutional division of the tasks and powers of government between the general government and the state governments. Within its sphere the general government is a complete national government, but that sphere is limited; and within their own spheres the states act as constitutionally independent entities.[51]

Initially it was the Anti-Federalists who doubted the viability of such a mixed system and the Federalists who affirmed it. The Anti-Federalists could not, however, maintain their strict federal ground, as we have seen, because they *did* see the Union as more than a league. Consequently they followed the Federalists into what we may call the "new federalism" (i.e., a mixed national and federal system) and, despite early misgivings, became its strongest advocates; for it seemed, under all the circumstances, the best way to preserve the principles they thought fundamental. At this point there is another shift. Once the legitimacy of the new federalism is accepted, the Federalists emphasized the primacy of the national component in the mixture, while the Anti-Federalists urged the importance of a strict division of power and even something like a divided sovereignty, the possibility of which their early strictly federal argument had denied.

Not surprisingly, these shifts were reflected in terminological confusion or ambiguity. Some of the Federalists deliberately contributed to this confusion by calling this new combination of federal and national government a "federal" government. The implication, which has some surface plausibility, is that nothing very substantial hinges on a shift from one "federal" mixture in the Articles of Confederation to another "federal" mixture in the Constitution.[52] Terminological confusion is also found on the Anti-Federal side. In the reasoning of The Federal Farmer, for example, there is an overall movement from the old federalism to the new, which is reflected in a very significant terminological shift. In his first essay, The Federal Farmer makes the traditional three-part distinction between a federal plan, a consolidation, and what he here calls "partial consolidation," which is a combination of federal and national elements. But in his sixth essay (in the Additional Letters) what he had formerly called "federal" becomes a form of "pretended federalism" and what was formerly called partial consolidation becomes the true or honest federalism.[53]

The notion that the general and the particular governments had different objects was of course not new. As we have seen, for example, Luther Martin had argued in the Philadelphia Convention that the state governments were to protect and regulate individual liberty, while the general government was formed to take care of essential common interests.[54] The Articles of Confederation were not a strictly federal system but a kind of mixture. But what was missing in the earlier view was a well-developed notion of *coordinate* jurisdictions and *coordinate* state and federal sovereigns. For Martin, the tasks of government were divided, but the states were supreme; for the nationalists, the tasks might be divided, but the national government would be supreme. In either of these views the tendency was to see any division of powers as a convenient arrangement sanctioned and subject to reassessment by the supreme power, whether that was the states or the general government. The Anti-Federalists could not consistently hold to the doctrine of state supremacy because they admitted it would lead to anarchy among the states. They could not accept national supremacy because they thought it would lead to centralized tyranny. To avoid both extremes is the somewhat dubious promise of the new federalism: to provide, somehow, for a government in which neither the whole nor the parts are supreme.*[55]

The problem that persistently threatens this arrangement is of course how to deal with the possibility of conflicts between these governments and their tasks. This was, again, not a new problem, but it became acute as the notion of coordinate governments came into focus. It is true that the theoretical force of the argument against divided sovereignty was at least blunted by the perfection of the notion of the constitution as fundamental law: sovereignty could thus remain with the people, who partition power among their agents as they see fit.[56] The Federalists typically argued that the Constitution provided a sufficient delineation of power and that no vital conflict need arise. "The road is broad enough," Oliver Ellsworth said; "but if two men will jostle each other, the fault is not in the road."[57] But the very breadth of the road, the lack of restriction on the powers of the general government, and its independence of the states, seemed to the Anti-Federalists to make jostling inevitable with the states likely to find themselves in the ditch. There are only two ways to deal with this problem. Either the possibility of jostling must be altogether eliminated, or the states must be given the constitutional muscle to protect themselves in a more or less permanent contest.

To avoid conflict would require a comprehensive and exact partition of powers between the state and the general governments. Nowhere was the problem stated so clearly and its implication so sharply drawn as in James Monroe's suppressed pamphlet:

To mark the precise point at which the powers of the general government shall cease, and that from whence those of the states shall commence, to poise them in such manner as to prevent either destroying the other, will require the utmost force of human wisdom and ingenuity. No possible ground of variance or even interference should be left, for there would the conflict commence, that might perhaps prove fatal to both.[58]

Any room for adjustment or disagreement is room for the whole equilibrium again to be drawn into question; and the tendency will be to assert the supremacy of either the states or the federal government, with the resulting tyranny of consolidation or anarchy of mere confederation. Under the ambiguous constitutional partition of powers there is great danger of this kind. But Monroe's demand was of course utterly unrealistic, as the Anti-Federalists, for all their calls for a fuller more precise apportionment, admitted. Does that not destroy, then, the whole enterprise of the new federalism? Will not a mixed system inevitably move from whatever equilibrium is originally set to one of its extremes? Perhaps so, ultimately, but there is yet another Anti-Federalist defense. If the jurisdictions or respective sovereignties of the general and the state governments cannot be so unambiguously drawn as to avoid any future uncertainties, perhaps those governments can be constructed and empowered and related in ways that ensure that the inevitable adjustments and conflicts will leave the main parties essentially intact and the system, the nation, in equilibrium.

In practice this would require, in the opinion of the Anti-Federalists, measures to ensure the continued independence and vigor of the states, which were missing from the Constitution. They objected to the absence of explicit reservations in behalf of states' rights. Without an express declaration "in favour of the legislative rights of the several states, by which their sovereignty over their own citizens within the state should be secured," the states would "be preserved only during the pleasure of Congress."[59] The states had, moreover, been deprived of the power of self-defense. The centralization of the taxing and military authorities would leave the states and the people defenseless against their national rulers. "My great objection to this Government is, that it does not leave us the means of defending our rights; or, of waging war against tyrants. . . . Have we the means of resisting disciplined armies, when our only defence, the militia is put into the hands of Congress?"*[60] Neither was the states' influence in the general government adequately secured. No real security was to be found in the Senate, which was not truly federal and over whose deliberations the states would have little influence.*[61] The states were to have no constitutional check on the actions of the general government. It was no use pointing, as James Wilson did, to the role of the states in forming the general government.[62] Formally the states might be indispensable to the existence of the general government, but what would really count was state participation in the *operation* of government, and there was to be none of this in the new scheme.[63] The decisive issue here was the power of taxation. When Governor Randolph referred to that power as the "soul" of the new government, Patrick Henry shrewdly replied that "they shall not have the soul of Virginia."[64] Under the Constitution the states would have no constitutional way of influencing the raising of the federal revenue and thus would be closed out from substantial influence on federal policy. The states would at the same time have to sustain themselves with whatever crumbs might be left after the general government had taken its fill. The old system of requisitions provided the states with a constitutional check on the general government and ensured their continued independence. As Henry explained, requisitions are attended with the advantage of "deliberation," and the states can correct "oppressive errors" of the general government.[65] Or as Hamilton put it, "If States are to deliberate on the mode, they will also deliberate on the object of the supplies, and will grant or not grant as they approve or disapprove of it."[66] The obvious problem is that while the system of requisitions secures the position of the states, it undermines that of the general government. Why not, then, many Anti-Federalists asked, make room in the system of revenue raising for both the national and the federal principles? Allow the general government an independent source of revenue by giving it an unlimited power to impose duties; but for any additional revenue require it to make requisitions on the states, imposing direct taxes of its own only where the states fail to comply with the requisition. This was one of the recommendatory amendments that facilitated the crucial Mas-

sachusetts ratification, and it was prominent in subsequent lists of recommendatory amendments. Without here following out the debate on this
question, it should be considered whether this arrangement, which would
have been widely accepted among the Anti-Federalists, would not have
been the mode of revenue raising most consistent with the "new
federalism," and what its rejection implies for the American "federal" system.

The whole issue of the new federalism, as the Anti-Federalists saw it, was
very clearly laid out in the quite theoretical discussion of A [Pennsylvania]
Farmer. He began with the conventional distinction between general and
local concerns. "The perfection of a federal republic consists in drawing the
proper line between those objects of sovereignty which are of a general
nature, and which ought to be vested in the federal government, and those
which are of a more local nature and ought to remain with the particular
governments. . . ." But this distinction is not sufficient; it depends on a
deeper one:

[A]ll that portion of a sovereignty which involves the common interest of all
the confederating states, and which cannot be exercised by the states in
their individual capacity without endangering the liberty and welfare of the
whole, ought to be vested in the general government, reserving such a
proportion of sovereignty in the state governments as would enable them to
exist alone, if the general government should fail either by violence or with
the common consent of the confederates; the states should respectively
have laws, courts, force, and revenues of their own sufficient for their own
security; they ought to be fit to keep house alone if necessary; if this be not
the case, or so far as it ceases to be so, it is a departure from a federal to a
consolidated government. . . .[67]

In this striking rule A [Pennsylvania] Farmer makes clear what is implicit
in the Anti-Federalist acceptance of the "new federalism." The distinction
between general and local concerns is *not* an adequate rule, for that does not
ensure the maintenance of the federal equilibrium. That equilibrium consists
rather in, on the one hand, a general government capable of dealing with
general interests and, on the other hand, local governments capable of
existing alone if necessary. To ensure the latter was the true reason (sometimes only vaguely understood) for the Anti-Federalist commitment to the
system of requisitions, to state military power, and to constitutional checks
by the states on the general government. This position has a good deal of
weight if federalism is to be anything but a common sense modification of
consolidated national government, maintained fundamentally at the discretion of that government. Yet there is an obvious difficulty; the demands of
the common interest are likely to come into conflict with the requirement
that the states be "fit to keep house alone if necessary." Indeed while it can
be plausibly held that conflicts between local interests and general interests
are in principle reconcilable, the localities being parts of one whole, the
conflict between the general interest and the capacity of the states to exist

36

alone may be utterly irreconcilable. In fact, under A [Pennsylvania] Farmer's clearheaded analysis the new federalism dissolves into the stark alternative of the old federalism versus consolidation. And it is fairly clear which way A [Pennsylvania] Farmer would go when the conflict appears. There is, it seems, finally no middle way between a federal or a consolidated government; and while he is willing to define a federal government as substantially more than a league, it is fundamentally a league. So, on the other side, while Publius is willing to define the American federal system as something less than a national government, it is for him fundamentally a national government.

To the extent that men become persuaded that supremacy can be divided between central and local governments, the new federalism becomes theoretically defensible. Such men in 1787 and 1788 were rare. To the extent, however, that men are willing to concern themselves with dividing powers among the governments and adjusting their relations, the ultimate theoretical dilemma can be fended off by a series of practical arrangements. There were many such men in 1788. They were typically not very sanguine about the long-range viability of such arrangements, so much praised by later generations of scholars, historians, and statesmen; but they saw no other course. The Federalists accepted it mainly because of the strength of federal feeling in the country. Some of them saw it as a reasonable, permanent basis of government, many of them as a more or less temporary arrangement in the course of building a genuine national government. The Anti-Federalists were more likely to accept it as a long-term basis of American government, as a way of bringing together, if not reconciling, their own conflicting principles. As their commitment to simple federalism was more equivocal than the Federalists' commitment to simple nationalism, so their commitment to the new federalism, whose very principle is equivocation, was greater.

5

The Federalist Reply

Most of the major Federalists spoke the language of the new federalism, and some were content to rest their defense of the Constitution on this ground. The general and the particular governments have their different spheres and objects; the Constitution has defined these spheres reasonably well; and there is reason to hope that future adjustments will preserve a healthy balance. The most able Federalists, however, had reservations not merely about the feasibility of the new federalism but about its underlying premises. Men like James Madison thought that the solution of the internal as well as the external problems of American government was to be found not fundamentally in an equilibrium between states and Union, even if that could be achieved, but in a properly organized and empowered American republic. This view was prominent in the Philadelphia debates. Explaining the Virginia plan, Edmund Randolph "observed that the general object was to provide a cure for the evils under which the U.S. labored; that in tracing these evils to their origin every man had found it in the turbulence and follies of democracy. . . ."[1] Later James Madison explicitly challenged the narrow view expressed by Roger Sherman that the objects of Union were confined to dealing with foreign powers and preventing disputes among the states. To these should be added, Madison said, "the necessity of providing more effectually for the security of private rights, and the steady dispensation of Justice. Interferences with these were evils which had more perhaps than anything else, produced this convention. Was it to be supposed that republican liberty could long exist under the abuses of it practiced in [some of] the states."[2] This argument denies the basic premise of the Anti-Federal position and of the new federalism, the presumed superiority of the small republic in securing individual liberty and domestic tranquillity. On the contrary, the trouble with small republics is not mainly that they are weak and need to confederate for external purposes; it is that they cannot perform adequately the very tasks they are supposed to be best at.[*3] The extended American republic organized under the Constitution, while surely necessary for defense and commercial prosperity, will also be able to do the internal work of free republican government better than the states or any ideal small republic could do it. There are two parts of this crucial Federalist argument, the first having to do with the characteristic problem of republican government and the second with its solution.

The Federalist Reply

The characteristic problem of republican government is, in the words of Publius, majority faction, which is the majority "united and actuated by some common impulse of passion, or of interest, adverse to the rights of other citizens, or to the permanent and aggregate interests of the community."[4] This is not the traditional problem of popular licentiousness leading to resistance of authority and anarchy. Majority faction is the particular danger of popular government precisely because under popular government majorities can tyrannize under the cover of law.[5] This does not mean that Publius and the Federalists opposed majorities—Publius makes clear that not all majorities are factious—or that they were, as is sometimes inferred, enemies of popular government.[6] They did often declare against democracy (or against "pure democracy"), but democracy was understood in such contexts as a corrupt or extreme form of popular government.[7] The Federalists were preoccupied with majority faction (or democracy, in some formulations) precisely because of their commitment to the kind of government of which majority faction is the characteristic evil. The point is, as Madison explained in a letter to Jefferson, that "wherever the real power in a Government lies, there is the danger of oppression. In our Governments the real power lies in the majority of the community, and the invasion of private rights is *chiefly* to be apprehended, not from acts of Government contrary to the sense of its constituents, but from acts in which the Government is the mere instrument of the major number of the Constituents."[8]

Among the opponents of the Constitution there was some equivocation over majority faction. A few argued for pure democracy: "America under [a government] purely democratical, would be rendered the happiest and most powerful nation in the universe. . . ."[9] A very few seemed to deny that there can be such a thing as majority tyranny. When Brutus defined tyrannical government as that which, instead of serving the public good, promotes "the happiness and aggrandisement of one, or a few," he seemed to suggest, by omission, that there can be no tyrannical government of the many, though on the whole it is more accurate to say that, while not denying the possibility of majority tyranny, he did not see any need to discuss it.[10] Governor Clinton perhaps came closest to a denial in principle of the very possibility of majority tyranny when he insisted that the only true definition of free government is that "the will of the people . . . is law."[11]

In general, however, the Anti-Federalists acknowledged the possibility of majority faction and the need to guard against it, even though this danger typically occupied a less conspicuous place in their catalogue of dangers than in that of the Federalists.*[12] Impressed as they were by the English "Real Whigs," or Commonwealthmen, as Caroline Robbins has called them, the Anti-Federalists had been taught by their own experience that there were other dangers than kings, lords, and magistrates. Few of them would have agreed with Burgh that to argue that "the representatives of the people be checked and clogged in promoting the interest of their con-

39

stituents" is like arguing that "there ought to be a check to prevent individ-uals from being too healthy, or too virtuous. . . ."[13] Government by the people or, in practice, majority rule was accepted by the Anti-Federalists as the foundation of free government in America;*[14] but (Cato to the contrary notwithstanding) majority rule was not generally thought to be the very definition of free government, because it can lead to unjust deprivations of individual liberty. This was, indeed, one of the reasons some of the Anti-Federalists wanted a bill of rights. Thus Agrippa met the Federalist denial that a bill of rights is necessary in a representative government by insisting that it would serve "to secure the minority against the usurpation and tyranny of the majority."[15] A [Maryland] Farmer made the point even more emphatically:

The truth is, that the rights of individuals are frequently opposed to the apparent interests of the majority—For this reason the greater the portion of political freedom in a form of government the greater the necessity of a bill of rights—Often the natural rights of an individual are opposed to the pre-sumed interests or heated passions of a large majority of democratic gov-ernment; if these rights are not clearly and expressly ascertained, the indi-vidual must be lost; and for the truth of this I appeal to every man who has borne a part in the legislative councils of America. In such government the tyranny of the legislative is most to be dreaded.[16]

Jackson Turner Main's disappointed estimate is "that less than half of the Anti-Federalist leaders had democratic inclinations, and that these were muted."*[17] But the terms of this estimate are vague in the extreme. It would be difficult to find a single articulate American of this period who did not have very significant democratic "inclinations"; yet there were very few whose democratic inclinations were not, in some significant sense, "muted." Gordon Wood, on the other hand, characterizes the Anti-Federalists as genuine populists, as "majoritarians with respect to the state legislatures," as "true champions of the most extreme kind of democratic and egalitarian politics expressed in the Revolutionary era."[18] But what precisely does this mean? There were very few "democrats" among the Anti-Federalist writers (or probably among Americans of any kind) if by that is meant those who believe simply that the will of the majority of the people is law and that that will ought to be exercised as directly and with as little restraint as possible.*[19] However, the Anti-Federalists *were* typically more democratic than the Federalists in the specific sense that they were less likely to see majority faction as the most dangerous and likely evil of popular government. They were inclined to think, with Patrick Henry, that harm is more often done by the tyranny of the rulers than by the licentious-ness of the people.*[20] Moreover, so far as there may be a threat of licen-tiousness, it is to be met in the same way, fundamentally, as the threat to tyranny: by the alert public-spiritedness of the small, homogeneous, self-governing community

To the Federalists, Henry's and the other Anti-Federalists' view of both the problem and the solution missed the main points. Having established the centrality to republican government of the problem of majority tyranny, the Federalists went on to challenge the Anti-Federalist preference for the small republic in all of the three essential aspects that we have considered.[21] Rather than attempting to secure the patriotic attachment and law-abidingness of the citizens through a small republic, the Federalists would bind the citizens to their polity by effective government and good administration. Rather than trying to secure responsibility through a numerous representation, the Federalists would stress the filtering effect of representation; they would accept the natural leadership of the influential few, attaching it to the government and directing it toward the public good. And finally, rather than trying to foster republican simplicity, virtue, and self-restraint, the Federalists would rely on the many diverse private gratifications available in the extended republic, with its spaciousness and opportunity, to make it unlikely that any faction (and particularly a majority faction) would have the inclination or opportunity to tyrannize over others. Let us consider each of these challenges to the Anti-Federalist position in turn.

The Anti-Federalists thought, as we have seen, that a large republic cannot attract the voluntary obedience of the people and is therefore driven to execute its resolutions by military force. In the words of The Federal Farmer, "the general government, far removed from the people, and none of its members elected oftener than once in two years, will be forgot or neglected, and its laws in many cases disregarded, unless a multitude of officers and military force be continually kept in view, and employed to enforce the execution of the laws, and to make the government feared and respected."[22] If a government of force is to be avoided, the bonds of political union must be woven from the strands of the natural human association.

The strongest principle of union resides within our domestic walls. The ties of the parent exceed that of any other; as we depart from home, the next general principle of union is amongst citizens of the same state, where acquaintance, habits, and fortunes, nourish affection, and attachment; enlarge the circle still further, and, as citizens of different states, though we acknowledge the same national denomination, we lose the ties of acquaintance, habits, and fortunes, and thus, by degrees, we lessen in our attachments, till, at length, we no more than acknowledge a sameness of species.[23]

Significantly, Alexander Hamilton used exactly this thought in the New York ratifying convention and in *The Federalist* to show that the states need not fear being undermined by the new general government because they will always enjoy the attachment of the people. Followed with some care, however, Hamilton's discussion points to the Federalist alternative to the small natural community.

It is a known fact in human nature that its affections are commonly weak in proportion to the distance or diffusiveness of the object. Upon the same principle that a man is more attached to his family than to his neighborhood, to his neighborhood than to the community at large, the people of each State would be apt to feel a stronger bias towards their local governments than towards the government of the Union; *unless the force of that principle should be destroyed by a much better administration of the latter.*[24]

What is presented here as the incidental and apparently unlikely possibility of a better federal administration turns out to be crucial. Hamilton later makes it clear that there is "a probability that the general government *will* be better administered than the particular governments," being composed of a more select group of men, with more information and free of the taint of faction.[25] Thus the advantages of the close-knit natural community in inspiring the trust and confidence of the people can be replaced by the attractive benefits of the more effective government of the large republic.

Indeed, the Federalists claimed that their opponents mistook the political ground of trust, confidence, and even public morality, which is not intimate government but effective government. It is "not generally true," Hamilton told the New York convention, "that a numerous representation [is] necessary to obtain the confidence of the people. The confidence of the people will easily be gained by a good administration. This is the true touchstone." Public attachment to government "is more strongly secured by a train of prosperous events, which are the result of wise deliberation and vigorous execution," to which large bodies are less competent than small ones.[26] Governments attract the confidence of the people in the long run by deserving it. This includes, among other things, giving effective support to the virtues that all admit are desirable. The qualities of industry, economy, honesty, and civic virtue, about which the Anti-Federalists preach so much, are in fact undermined by the kind of governments the Anti-Federalists defend. Tender laws and paper money, the products of weak government, had led in America to well-known (and, by most Anti-Federalists, admitted) evils. "If virtue is the foundation of republican government, has it not been fatally sapped by these means? The morals of the people have been almost sunk into depravity; and the government of laws has been almost superseded by a licentious anarchy."[27] The crucial need, even for those who are the immediate losers, is wise and effective government and the confidence that only such a government can inspire. This is the source of civic prosperity. "The circulation of confidence is better than the circulation of money," and the pump of confidence is sound government, not government close to the people.

An aspect of any good government is a capacity to coerce obedience when necessary. To that extent the Anti-Federalists were right in saying that the new government would rest ultimately on force; they were wrong, in the Federalists' opinion, in thinking that there is any other kind. "[A]ll government is a kind of restraint" and "founded in force," Charles Pinckney told the South Carolina House of Representatives; "he could not conceive that either the dignity of a government could be maintained, its safety ensured, or its laws administered, without a body of regular forces to aid the magistrate in the execution of his duty."[28] Coercion also has a broader moral and political effect. "While it compels the obedience of the refractory, it redoubles the alertness of the virtuous by inspiring a confidence in the impartiality of its burthens."[29]

The Federalist view, then, was that an effective government, in addition to being intrinsically desirable, is also the key to the attachment of the people and to civic virtue itself. A government that can actually accomplish its resolves, that can keep the peace, protect property, and promote the prosperity of the country, will be a government respected and obeyed by its citizens. It will, moreover, promote private and public morality by providing them with effective protection.

The second element of the Federalist solution of the problem of popular government is a proper system of representation. In the main, the Anti-Federalists accepted representation reluctantly, as a necessary device in a community where the people cannot assemble to do their common business. The representative body is seen in consequence as a substitute for an assembly of all the citizens, which ought to be as like the whole body as possible. The Federalists, on the other hand, saw representation not as an unfortunate necessity but as an opportunity. It permits, in the first place, an extension of popular government. Through representation, especially in a federal system, "the people of a large country may be represented as truly as those of a small one."[30] Representation is the device that makes the large republic possible. But it is more. Arguing that representation was not new, but was put to a new use in the American governments, Publius made the striking observation that the difference between ancient governments and the American governments lay "*in the total exclusion of the people in their collective capacity* from any share in the *latter*, and not in the *total exclusion of representatives of the people*, from the administration of the former.*" To secure the full effect of this benefit, however, it must be connected to an extensive territory. "For it cannot be believed that any form of representative government, could have succeeded within the narrow limits occupied by the democracies of Greece."*[31] Thus representation is necessary to secure the benefits of the large republic; but the large republic is also necessary to secure the benefits of representation. These benefits are to be found, negatively expressed, in the capacity of a representative system to provide for a popular government in which the people collectively play no part and in which the danger of popular excesses is thereby reduced. As a Virginia Federalist argued, "the more independent a government is . . . of the people, under proper restraints," the more likely it is to produce the security of persons and property which is the end of government.[32]

As we have seen, the Anti-Federalists complained that in a large republic the people will not in practice be able to choose men like themselves, and

the representative body will inevitably be composed of the natural aristocracy. In large districts, "a common man must ask a man of influence how he
is to proceed, and for whom he must vote," and the only men with a chance
of being elected are those of "conspicuous military, popular, civil or legal
talents."[33] The Federalists replied that it is inevitable and natural that the
people should choose such men to represent them; they cannot and should
not be prevented from doing so. The small manufacturer sees that the merchant can represent him in public councils better than he could represent
himself. The small landholder sees that his basic interests are shared with
and protected by the great landholder. And what is wrong with electing men
of conspicuous talents? Who composes this "natural aristocracy" before
which the opponents of the Constitution tremble? They are the most distinguished, the most trusted, the most able men (and that is, on the whole, how
the Anti-Federalists themselves identified them). But are not these precisely
the kinds of men who ought to be the people's representatives? Even the
radical constitution of Pennsylvania, James Wilson pointed out, declared
that "representatives should consist of those most noted for wisdom and
virtue." "If this is [what is] meant by a natural aristocracy, and I know no
other, can it be objectionable that men should be employed that are most
noted for their virtue and talents?"*[34] In New York, Chancellor Livingston
argued against rotation on the same grounds. It is "an absurd species of
ostracism—a mode of proscribing eminent merit, and banishing from sta-
tions of trust those who have filled them with the greatest faithfulness."
Moreover, should not virtue and talents be encouraged by honors and re-
wards? "The acquisition of abilities is hardly worth the trouble, unless one
is to enjoy the satisfaction of employing them for the good of one's country."[35]

Thus the positive side of the Federalist case for representation is the
likelihood that it will produce a government with a capacity to govern well.
The probability is increased in an extensive republic, which is more likely to
put forward "proper guardians of the public weal" and less susceptible to
electoral corruption than a small one. Corruption is difficult where there are
many to bribe, and the large district is protection against other forms of
"bribery" such as demagoguery and appeals to narrow interests.[36] Petty
republics and small districts are the natural homes of petty men. "It is only
in remote corners of a government," James Wilson thought, "that little
demagogues arise. Nothing but real weight of character, can give a man real
influence over a large district."[37] In a large district an aspiring politician has
to seek a wide base of support, and this increases the likelihood of his taking
a broad view or at least decreases the chances of narrow partiality. "The
little demagogue of a petty parish or county will find his importance annihi-
lated, and his intrigues useless, when several counties join in an election; he
probably would not be known, certainly not regarded, out of his own circle;
while the man whose abilities and virtue had extended a fair reputation

beyond the limits of his county, would, nine times out of ten, be the person who would be the choice of the people."*[38] For the Federalists, then, representation is a mode of selecting for rulers the best men, or at least men better than average; and the large districts of the large republic increases the chance of securing such men.

Consistently with this view that, as Publius said, the first aim of every constitution should be "to obtain for rulers men who possess most wisdom to discern, and most virtue to pursue, the common good of the society," the Federalists saw the duty of representatives as extending beyond the particular interests of their constituents to the common good.*[39] Noah Webster said, for example, that while a delegate is bound to represent "the true local interest" of those who elect him, "when each provincial interest is thus stated, every member should act for the *aggregate interest* of the whole confederacy. The design of representation is to bring the collective interest into view. . . ."[40] The Federalists were not naïve about the tendencies of representatives to act for narrow and selfish views; but the aim was a system in which the collective interest will emerge. Representation is not sufficient, but it is the basic device through which the people not merely re-presents but transcends itself. As Fisher Ames put it, "the representation of the people is something more than the people."*[41]

Against the third part of the Anti-Federalist defense of the small republic, the need for republican simplicity and public-spiritedness, the Federalists put forward the diversity of the extended commercial republic. Most of the Anti-Federalists thought, with Brutus, that "in a republic, the manners, sentiments, and interests of the people should be similar. If this is not the case, there will be a constant clashing of opinions; and the representatives of one part will be continually striving against those of the other."[42] The Federalists contended that such a homogeneous republic was possible only under the primitive, harsh conditions of a precommercial society, which no man—certainly no American—would choose to endure. John Adams had made the point well in his discussion of the little republic of San Marino.

A handful of poor people, living in the simplest manner, by hard labor, upon the produce of a few cows, sheep, goats, swine, poultry and pigeons, on a piece of rocky, snowy ground, protected from every enemy by their situation, their superstition, and even by their poverty, having no commerce nor luxury, can be no example for the commonwealth of Pennsylvania, Georgia, or Vermont, in one of which there are possibly half a million of people, and in each of the others at least thirty thousand, scattered over a large territory.[43]

A safe mediocrity can be maintained in conditions like those of San Marino; but "in every community where industry is encouraged, there will be a division of it into the few and the many."*[44] And when this occurs, the innocence of the primitive community is lost. The Anti-Federalists could not deny this; yet they did not really desire the simple, precommercial society, even if they could have had it. It is true that they criticized the man of commerce, "immersed in schemes of wealth" and thus "the last to take the alarm when public liberty is threatened."[45] He has no permanent attachments and can pack up and move, leaving the farmer to suffer the consequences of a bad constitution. But this was the half-hearted criticism of children of the modern commercial world who worried about its implications. There was no attempt to articulate an alternative, no account of the virtue of the agrarian way of life. There was some hankering after a simple, subsistence agricultural life, but the Anti-Federalists were irrevocably committed to a commercial order, as indeed American agriculture had always been.[46] The Federalists drew out the implications of the commitment. While they were about as likely as their opponents to write as "Farmer" or "Countryman," they denied that there was any real conflict between the landed and the commercial interests, because (as they suggested more or less explicitly) the American landed interest is fundamentally part of and dependent upon the commercial order. The Federalist Landholder argued, for example, "It may be assumed as a fixed truth that the prosperity and riches of the farmer must depend on the prosperity, and good national regulation of trade. Artful men may insinuate the contrary— tell you let trade take care of itself, and excite your jealousy against the merchant because his business leads him to wear a gayer coat, than your economy directs. But let your own experience refute such insinuations."*[47] The American world is the world of commerce.

The basic problem of the Anti-Federalists was that they accepted the need and desirability of the modern commercial world, while attempting to resist certain of its tendencies with rather half-hearted appeals to civic virtue. But such restraints, the Federalists replied, have never worked and will never work; the solution is to be found in another direction entirely.

Virtue, patriotism, or love of country, never was and never will be, till mens' natures are changed, a fixed, permanent principle and support of government. But in an agricultural country, a general possession of land in fee simple, may be rendered perpetual, and the inequalities introduced by commerce, are too fluctuating to endanger government. An equality of property, with a necessity of alienation, constantly operating to destroy combinations of powerful families, is the very *soul of a republic*.[48]

To this James Madison added the extended republic.*[49] For even in the absence of primogeniture and under the constant churning of commerce distinct interests will eventually form and find their way into the political realm. Despite unparalleled opportunity for individual enterprise, the time will come even under American conditions where the many will resent the greater goods enjoyed by the few. And in a popular government where the majority are united by a common interest or passion the rights of the minority are in danger. "The only remedy is to enlarge the sphere, & thereby divide the community into so great a number of interests & parties, that in the 1st place a majority will not be likely at the same moment to have a common interest separate from that of the whole or of the minority; and in the 2d place, that in case they shd. have such an interest, they may not be apt to unite in the pursuit of it. It was incumbent on us then to try this remedy, and with that view to frame a republican system on such a scale and in such a form as will controul all the evils wch. have been experienced."[50] What Brutus saw as a great defect of the Constitution—that the legislature "would be composed of such heterogeneous and discordant principles, as would constantly be contending with each other"[51]—James Madison and others saw as its greatest virtue. In a large, diverse, wealthy country men can find ample opportunity to gratify their private wants; they will be less likely to resent the success and to encroach on the rights of others, and such resentment as they do feel will be less likely to take dangerous political form. "Divide et impera," the reprobated axiom of tyranny, is, under certain qualifications, the only policy by which a republic can be administered on just principles.[52]

The trouble with the Anti-Federalists, in this view, was that they saw civil society as a teacher, as a molder of character, rather than as a regulator of conduct. Their mentality was like that expressed in a 1776 proclamation of the Massachusetts General Court:

That piety and virtue, which alone can secure the freedom of any people, be encouraged, and vice and immorality suppressed, the Great and General Court have thought fit to issue this Proclamation, commanding and enjoining it upon the good people of this colony that they lead sober, religious, and peacable lives, avoiding all blasphemies, contempt of the Holy Scriptures and of the *Lord's* Day, and all other crimes and misdemeanors, all debauchery, profaneness, corruption, venality, all riotous and tumultuous proceedings and all immoralities whatsoever, and that they decently and reverently attend the publick worship of God.[53]

Preaching like this, whether in the form of a direct injunction or the supposed functioning of the small republic, seemed to the Federalists ineffective, or at least grossly insufficient. No matter how strong the preaching or the community surveillance, men's interests will not be subdued or governed by considerations of public good, moral duty, or religious salvation.*[54] To warnings like that of Anti-Federalist Thomas Wait that to try to subject the vast continent of America to a democracy would be as futile as trying "to rule Hell by Prayer,"[55] the Federalist reply was, in effect, that little democracies can no more be ruled by prayer than large ones. Men act mainly from passion and interest. The Constitution was deliberately and properly designed not to try to stifle or transform those motives—to try to rule them by prayer—but to channel them in the direction of the public good.

6
The Aristocratic Tendency of the Constitution

The Federalist argument that we have been considering rejects as unrealistic the traditional republican reliance on patriotism, on respect for reputation, on the restraints of conscience, even on the not very elevated principle that honesty is the best policy. It relies instead on a constitutional system within which the strongest natural forces—particularly the passion of acquisitiveness or avarice—are not stifled (a hopeless endeavor) but are guided into channels conducive to the public good, or channels that at least make it extremely difficult for anyone to tyrannize over anyone else. The chief source of danger is always whatever element of society enjoys the right to rule, because it can tyrannize without usurpation. In republican government the problem is thus to prevent a tyranny of the majority or the many. The small republic cannot solve this problem; the well-constituted large republic can. Part of that solution lies, however, in a large, powerful government, even though that aspect of the solution is not prominent in Madison's classic formulation. For the Anti-Federalists that government is seen as itself the major problem.

More precisely the Anti-Federalists see the chief danger as the inherently aristocratic character of any government. All government is, more or less, government of the many by the few. This aristocratic character of organized civil society tends to become more severe and more selective over time, and the main efforts of constitution makers should be directed to at least putting obstacles in its way. The powerful, irresponsible government under the proposed Constitution, on the contrary, will hasten this tendency. "It changes, totally changes, the form of your present government. From a well-digested, well-formed democratic, you are at once rushing into an aristocratic government."[1] This is the underlying theme of a vast quantity of the specific criticism by the Anti-Federalists of the proposed Constitution.*[2]

Thus, so far as the proposed legislature was concerned, the Anti-Federalists criticized the House of Representatives, as we have seen, for providing only a shadow of representation; but their strongest indignation was reserved for the Senate, which represented for many of them all that was wrong with the Constitution. While seldom denying the need for a select body to check the excesses of the more popular assembly, they did object to giving this less popular branch of the legislature most of the critical powers of government. The mixture of legislative, executive, and judicial

48

powers in the Senate violated the maxim of separation and seemed designed to lay the foundation for a permanent aristocracy.*[3] "[W]e have seen powers, in every branch of government, in violation of all principle, and all safety condensed in this aristocratic senate: we have seen the representative, or democratic branch, weakened exactly in proportion to the strengthening the aristocratic. . . ." The Senate was the "great efficient body" of this new government and the fetus of an aristocratic domination.[4]

The same theme runs through the Anti-Federalists' criticisms of the executive, though there was more ambiguity here than might be expected. Many Anti-Federalists thought that a unitary executive was necessary, for the sake of both efficiency and responsibility, and agreed with The Federal Farmer that the office of the President and the mode of his election were well conceived. There was a fair amount of sympathy for a strong (even, under some circumstances, a hereditary) executive to resist the aristocratic tendencies of the legislature; and some of the Anti-Federalists objected that the President would be too weak to stand up to the Senate and would become a mere tool of aristocratic domination.[5] The Federal Farmer went so far as to justify a strong executive as providing that unifying "first man" that even republics need.*[6] The more common Anti-Federal view, however, was a rather pedestrian hostility to a strong executive. Some continued to argue in favor of a plural executive or an executive council, as Randolph and Mason had done in Philadelphia, to avoid the danger of monarchy and dominance by one section.*[7] Many objected that with his veto, his powers as commander-in-chief, his powers of appointment, and his general authority to see that the laws are faithfully executed, the "President-General"—as many of them called him, after the executive officer in the Galloway Plan of Union in 1774—could find justification for almost anything he might wish to do.[8] Young William Symmes shrewdly anticipated the grounds of later Presidential expansion.

But was ever a commission so *brief,* so *general,* as this of our President? Can we exactly say how far a faithful execution of the laws may extend? or what may be called or comprehended in a faithful execution? If the President be guilty of a misdemeanor, will he not take care to have this excuse? And should it turn against him, may he not plead a mistake! or is he bound to understand the laws, or their operation? Should a Federal law happen to be as generally expressed as the President's authority; must he not interpret the Act! For in many cases he must execute the laws independent of any judicial decision. And should the legislature direct the mode of executing the laws, or any particular law, is he obliged to comply, if he does not think it will amount to a faithful execution? For to suppose that the legislature can make laws to affect the office of President, is to destroy his independence, and in this case to supersede the very constitution. Is there no instance in which he may reject the sense of the legislature, and establish his own, and so far, would he not be to all intents and purposes absolute?[9]

Better, said Patrick Henry, a dictator in times of need, like the one we had in 1781, who was chosen for his personal qualities and who rendered up his power after using it gloriously, rather than this American presidency which can scarcely be expected to be filled by a train of such men.[10]

In the Constitutional provisions for the judiciary, too, the Anti-Federalists thought they saw the tracks of a consolidating aristocracy. The weakening of the place of the jury, the provision for a complete system of national courts, the extensive jurisdiction of the national judiciary, the provision for appeal to the Supreme Court on questions of fact as well as law, and the supremacy of the Constitution and the laws and treaties made thereunder all seemed to give enormous power over the vital daily concerns of men to a small group of irresponsible judges.[11] Although the broadest reaches of the judiciary, described subsequently by Hamilton and Marshall, were seldom canvassed during the ratification debates, the Anti-Federalists glimpsed enough to make them wary.*[12] The most farsighted of them, Brutus, very accurately anticipated the breadth with which the Supreme Court would construe its own powers and those of the general legislature and the line of reasoning that would be used. "I question whether the world ever saw, in any period of it, a court of justice invested with such immense powers, and yet placed in a situation so little responsible." Brutus predicted, moreover, the judicial review of acts of Congress and the consequent supremacy of an irresponsibile judiciary. "If . . . the legislature pass any laws, inconsistent with the sense the judges put upon the constitution, they will declare it void; and therefore in this respect their power is superior to that of the legislature."[13] The Federal Farmer joined Brutus in trying to show that the federal judiciary was a threat not only to state courts and to individuals but to the regime as a whole. Americans, accustomed to look to courts as checks on legislative and executive excesses, had forgotten their inherent arbitrariness. "We are not sufficiently attentive to the circumstances, that the measures of popular legislatures naturally settle down in time, and gradually approach a mild and just medium; while the rigid systems of the law courts naturally become more severe and arbitrary, if not carefully tempered and guarded by the constitution, and by laws, from time to time." Indeed, The Federal Farmer concluded—in direct contradiction to Publius' later contention that the judiciary was politically the "least dangerous" department—that "we are more in danger of sowing the seeds of arbitrary government in this department than in any other."*[14] Thus some Anti-Federalists saw the general judiciary as a locus from which an irresponsible aristocracy of legal skill might gradually and irresistibly encroach on the more popular parts of government, an anticipation of more recent concerns about the implications of legal rationality and bureaucratization.

In reply to all of these objections, the Anti-Federalists complained, they were told, "trust your rulers; they will be good men." According to the Federalists, Centinel said, "a good administration will atone for all the defects in the government, which, say they, you must necessarily have, for how can it be otherwise, your rulers are to be taken from among yourselves."[15] A considerable amount of Anti-Federalist heat on this subject was generated by Judge Thomas McKean, who was reported to have said in the Pennsylvania ratifying convention that "though a good system is certainly a blessing, yet the wealth, the prosperity, and the freedom of the people, must ultimately depend upon the administration of the best government. The wisdom, probity and patriotism of the rulers, will ever be the criterion of public prosperity; and hence it is, that despotism, if well administered, is the best form of government invented by human ingenuity."*[16] Few Federalists went so far. Indeed, their principal argument was precisely that the interior arrangements of the Constitution were premised on a very realistic view of the untrustworthiness of rulers and cautiously provided "by opposite and rival interests, the defect of better motives." In the new system, "interest and integrity will be connected by the closest ties."[17] Nevertheless all the Federalists insisted that there must be some degree of confidence in rulers. Some relied heavily on the wisdom and virtue of the men they expected to be in charge of the new government. Thus a Federalist writer in Georgia contended that "none will be distinguished with places of trust but those who possess superior talents and accomplishments. . . ." Cassius, in a reply to Richard Henry Lee, argued that the House of Representatives would consist of men "of unsullied reputations;—of men, in whose bosoms the *sacred* principle of patriotism has, *always,* glowed in its utmost purity;—of men, who, in every possible situation of affairs, have, *invariably,* discovered an uncorruptible attachment to their country. . . ."[18] More commonly, however, the Federalist position was that jealousy of rulers must be kept within some kind of bounds, and not "extended to a degree which is degrading and humiliating to human nature. . . ."[19] "It is said that there ought to be jealousy in mankind," said Iredell. "I admit it as far as is consistent with prudence; but unlimited jealousy is very pernicious."[20] "[M]ean jealousy and groundless distrusts . . . in some measure authorize [our representatives] to betray their trust. . . ."[21] In the balanced terms of Publius, "the supposition of universal venality in human nature is little less an error in political reasoning than the supposition of universal rectitude. The institution of delegated power implies that there is a portion of virtue and honor among mankind, which may be a reasonable foundation of confidence."[22]

Nevertheless the extent to which the Federalists were willing to rely on the virtue and honor of the rulers seemed to the Anti-Federalists foolish or suspicious. A wise people will never place themselves in the hands of arbitrary government in the hopes that it will be virtuous. "Let us not flatter ourselves that we shall always have good men to govern us." The Spirit of '76 was not trust in rulers. "Confidence," Elbridge Gerry said in Philadelphia, "is the road to tyranny.*[23] Of course no one denied that confidence is a necessary part of representative government (though it could be argued that that is precisely one of the reasons why representative government is so problematical), and the Anti-Federalists wanted to provide a basis for a reasonable degree of confidence by, among other things, increasing the representation in the House of Representatives. But public office tends to attract bad men and to bring out the worst in good ones. "[C]onstitutions are not so necessary to regulate the conduct of good rulers as to restrain that of bad ones." "Scruples would be impertinent," Robert Lansing told the New York convention, "arguments would be in vain, checks would be useless, if we were certain our rulers would be good men; but for the virtuous government is not instituted: its object is to restrain and punish vice; and all free constitutions are formed with two views—to deter the governed from crime, and the governors from tyranny." And while the Anti-Federalists, with Melancton Smith, would not affirm that all men are dishonest, in forming a constitution it is well to be on the safe side and assume that they are.*[24]

The irony is that whereas "the primary object of government" is "to check and controul the ambitious and designing," government tends to become itself the tool of these very men. Thus the overriding concern of the founder, the statesman, and the alert citizen should be the danger of insidious usurpation by the few, the inevitable and persistent pressure of "the artful and ever active aristocracy."[25] If the people will not or cannot govern themselves, the few will do it; and the fact is that the people generally cannot govern themselves, at least not outside their small communities, which is another argument for the small republic.[26] The few never sleep, while the many are rarely truly awake. "The aristocracy," said A [Maryland] Farmer, "who move by system and design, and always unde; the colourable pretext of securing property, act as has been frequently said like the screw in mechanics, always gaining, holding fast what it gains, and never loosing; and in the event has ever proved an overmatch for the multitude, who never act but from their feelings, and are never permitted to feel *until it is too late. . . .*"[27] Were the people always attentive, they could call unfaithful lawmakers home and send others; but they are not always attentive. Thus except under the rare circumstances of the small, homogeneous republic (and perhaps even then) rigorous provision for popular responsibility is not sufficient. "Virtue will slumber," Patrick Henry warned. "The wicked will be continually watching: Consequently you will be undone."*[28]

7

Complex Government

A people can protect themselves, with what ultimate effect remains uncertain, from their own neglectful slumber and the encroachment of the watchful few through properly formed constitutions.[1] Through limited grants of power, tight responsibility, and internal checks, the few may be prevented from doing much harm while the people drowse or pursue their private lives. But it is important to do the job properly while the people are attentive, and this is why the Anti-Federalists distrusted proposals to ratify the Constitution in expectation of future amendments. "[W]e are to expect the ardour of many, yea, of most people, will be abated;—their exertions will cease, or be languid, and they will sit down easy, although they may see that the constitution . . . does not sufficiently guard the rights of the people, or secure them against the encroachments of their rulers." They will consider the work done and neglect their liberties. "Besides, the human mind cannot continue intensely engaged for any great length of time upon one object. As after a storm, a calm generally succeeds, so after the minds of a people have been ardently employed upon a subject, especially upon that of government, we commonly find that they become cool and inattentive. . . ." Future amendments are a weak reliance. "The deed is executed—the conveyance is made—and the power of reassuming the right is gone, without the consent of the parties.—Besides, when a government is once in operation, it acquires strength by habit, and stability by exercise."[2] Before the labyrinth of amendment can be traced, "perhaps the great principles upon which our late glorious revolution was founded, will be totally forgotten."[3]

The great principle of the revolution can be expressed for present purposes as the doctrine of limited government. The Federalists and Anti-Federalists agreed that government is properly directed to the pursuit of limited ends, namely the security of individual rights; and there was very little debate about limited government in this fundamental sense, although, as we have seen, the Anti-Federalists thought the defenders of the Constitution sometimes exceeded these limits.[4] But the chief concern of limited government for the Founding generation was with subordinate limits on governmental action. And here differences begin. The first of these subordinate limits is responsibility to the people. The second is limited powers. These were the major concern of the Anti-Federalists, as we have seen, and for many they were all that mattered. To this attitude the Federalists' impatient and powerful rejoinder was that it is not sufficient to talk of the dangers of the powers granted when all admit that broad powers are necessary, or to hark back to direct popular responsibility when all agree that a simple democracy would be both impracticable and positively undesirable. The way to limit government effectively is not by niggardly grants of power—which can only result in a government incapable of doing its work except by violating the Constitution—or by simple structure—which can only invite tyranny—but by a properly designed complex internal structure.

In the Federalists' view, one of the Founders' supreme achievements was the construction of a marvelous limited government in this third and crucial sense. Thus Alexander Hamilton argued in the New York Convention that the system of checks and balances in the Constitution "is so complex, so skilfully contrived, that it is next to impossible that an impolitic or wicked measure should pass the scrutiny with success."[5] But where Hamilton saw a finely wrought clock, the Anti-Federalists saw darkness and danger. They found the Constitution inexplicit, obscure, and dangerously complex. "A constitution," Patrick Henry said, "ought to be, like a beacon, held up to the public eye, so as to be understood by every man." But "this government is of such an intricate and complicated nature, that no man on this earth can know its real operation."[6] "[W]here is the man who can see through the constitution to its effects?" another Anti-Federalist asked. "The constitution of a wise and free people, ought to be as evident to simple reason, as the letters of our alphabet—."[7] The Constitution did not establish any identifiable *kind* of government. It was illegitimate as well as obscure. Again and again, the Anti-Federalists spat out their scorn of this "spurious brat," "this bantling," this "13 horned monster," "this heterogeneous phantom."[8] "What kind of government is this?" asked Patrick Henry. "Is this a Monarchy, like England—a compact between Prince and people; with checks on the former, to secure the liberty of the latter? Is this a Confederacy, like Holland—an association of a number of independent States, each of which retain its individual sovereignty? It is not a democracy, wherein the people retain all their rights securely."[9] The "favoured bantling" would have had no name, even, had not James Wilson, "in the fertility of his genius, suggested the happy epithet of a *Federal Republic*."[10]

Yet if the government had been truly a federal government, no complex internal checks would have been necessary. Luther Martin explained "that a *federal government* is formed by the *States,* as *States* that is in their *sovereign* capacities, in the same manner as *treaties* and *alliances* are formed—That a *sovereignty* considered as such, cannot be said to have jarring interests or principles, the one aristocratic, and the other democratic; but that the principles of a *sovereignty* considered as a sovereignty, are the *same*, whether that sovereignty is monarchical, aristocratical, democratical, or mixed—."[11] As we have seen, however, most of the Anti-Federalists admitted the need for something other than a federal government for the United States, and they admitted in consequence the need for a structure more complex than an assembly of sovereigns.*[12] Indeed, it is striking that while the Anti-Federalists often defended the pre-eminent place of the states in the general government formed by the Articles of Confederation and its very limited powers, they very seldom defended the absence from that government of any differentiation of functions or internal checks.

We come, then, to the question of the structure of the government. Cecelia Kenyon is generally correct in saying that the Anti-Federalists favored a system of separation of powers and checks and balances and would have dissented from the view that checks and balances are incompatible with genuine popular government.[13] The Anti-Federalists typically criticized the Constitution because there was too little separation, not too much, and too few checks, not too many. Yet it is not quite accurate to say, as Kenyon does, that no one among the Anti-Federalists "attacked the general validity of the system of separation of powers and checks and balances." The full explanation is more complex.

One of the major Anti-Federalist statements, the first essay by Centinel, does in fact contain a vigorous attack on the very principle of checks and balances.[14] Centinel chose for his target John Adams, whose discussion of balanced government was probably the best preconstitutional treatment of this matter and was considered by Centinel to have been influential among the Philadelphia delegates.*[15] While considering the differences between Adams and the Anti-Federalists, however, we shall also need to see that in their understanding of balanced government they stand together in contrast to the great theoreticians of the Constitution, such as James Madison and James Wilson. "Mr. Adams's *sine qua non* of a good government," Centinel wrote, "is three balancing powers whose repelling qualities are to produce an equilibrium of interests, and thereby promote the happiness of the whole community." Adams' view is that the governors will always be actuated by self-interest and therefore that it is necessary "to create an opposition of interests between the members of two distinct bodies, in the exercise of the powers of government, and balanced by those of a third."[16] According to Adams—and we are no longer relying on Centinel's report— there have been only three discoveries in the constitution of free govern-ment since the time of Lycurgus: "representation, instead of collections of the people; a total separation of the executive from the legislative power, and of the judicial from both; and a balance in the legislature, by three independent, equal branches. . . ."[17] The issue of representation need not concern us at present. The other two modern discoveries are of the utmost importance for the present discussion. As we shall see, the Anti-Federalists accepted and advocated a separation of legislative, executive, and judicial powers (or functions) and a system of checks and balances among them to maintain the separation and to avoid a concentration of power. But Adams' "balance" is essentially a balance within the legislature, and more important it is a balance of "orders" in the community—not hereditary orders but the natural arrangements of many, few, and one. This view cuts across and gets intertwined with the notion of a separation of the legislative, executive, and judicial functions; but the basic concern is with the balance of the different parts of the community, their different interests, and their different claims to rule, whether those parts are king, lords, commons; the many and the few; or any other fundamental differentiation.[18] This approach grows out of the great tradition of the mixed regime.*[19] As we shall see, the major Federalist theoreticians sharply modified or even abandoned this approach, providing a new statement of the whole issue of balanced government. Before considering this, however, we need to pursue further the Anti-Federalists' disagreement with Adams. For it is here, more than in their responses to specific provisions of the Constitution, that their own view of the question of "mixed" or "complex" or "balanced" government becomes most clear.

What is crucial for this purpose is that Adams directly and explicitly rejects the idea of simple government. Centinel, on the other hand, advocates simple government, and most of the Anti-Federalists were at least inclined in that direction, despite all their participation in the discussion about balances. Centinel contends that a system such as Adams' is beyond the wisdom of man to establish and maintain and that it would in any case not accomplish its objectives. "If the administrators of every government are actuated by views of private interest and ambition, how is the welfare and happiness of the community to be the result of such jarring adverse interests?" The true principle—or perhaps it would be better to say the pure or primary principle—of free government is not balance but responsibility. "I believe it will be found that the form of government, which holds those entrusted with power, in the greatest responsibility to their constituents, the best calculated for freemen." A republican or free government can only exist where the people are virtuous and property evenly distributed; "in such a government the people are the sovereign and their sense or opinion is the criterion of every public measure; for when this ceases to be the case, the nature of government is changed, and an aristocracy, monarchy or despotism will rise on its ruin."[20] This is of course a version of the argument for the small republic that we have considered above. Responsibility is best attained in a government of simple structure, under which the people can quickly and easily identify the source of abuse. Complex governments, A [Maryland] Farmer argued, "seem to bid defiance to all responsibility, (the only true test of good government) as it can never be discovered where the fault lies. . . ."[21]

If this is a basic Anti-Federalist position, or at least tendency, why was it not more often explicitly put forward? Why did the Anti-Federalists spend most of their time arguing about the inadequacy of the checks and balances provided in the Constitution rather than taking a firm stand for simple and responsible government? Part of the reason is that the conditions for simple government did not exist in the case of the general government; but there is a deeper problem, which is connected with the aristocratic tendency of government that we have already discussed.[22] The case for simple government never seems to be squarely put, either in theory or in practice. The extraordinary men, who have an interest in great, enterprising, ambitious government, are in control of both the councils of state and the theory books.

Is it . . . possible that governments of simplicity and equal right, can have been fairly dealt by in theory or practice? The votaries of tyranny and usurpation stand not alone—in bitter opposition; every man of enterprize, or superior talents and fortune, is interested to debase them; their banners have ever been deserted because they never can pay their troops.—The most amiable and sensible of mankind seems to have made a stand in favour of a mixed government, founded on the permanent orders and objects of men. Thither I suspect the American government is now tending. If it must be so—Let it go gently then—with slow and equal steps.[23]

It is almost as if the fate of simple government is sealed once simple government is questioned or challenged—which means whenever any man exercises his greater ambition, or wisdom, or virtue. As the Anti-Federalists saw an inevitable aristocratic impulse in civil society, so they saw an irresistible tendency toward complex government. And however much they regretted it—and unlike the Federalists they did regret it—they saw more or less the necessity of accepting this tendency and putting it to the service of liberty. John Adams stressed that there are numerous sources of inequality even in America, arising from differences "founded in the constitution of nature" in wealth, talents, and family background. These differences give rise to a "natural aristocracy," which "forms a body of men which contains the greatest collection of virtues and abilities in a free government, is the brightest ornament and glory of the nation, and may always be made the greatest blessing of society, if it be judiciously managed in the constitution." But the natural aristocracy must be managed; otherwise it is dangerous and cannot fail to lead to the destruction of the commonwealth. The instrument of management is a carefully designed complex government.[24] However tempting the Anti-Federalists found Turgot's contention that complex government was unnecessary in America because there were no fixed orders and all men were equal, they saw the force of Adams' rebuttal. Thus A [Maryland] Farmer, one of the strongest advocates among the Anti-Federalists of simple government, was driven to conclude that the great task of a free people is to manage and control the natural aristocracy. "In fine, in all governments by *representation* or *delegation of power*, where property is secured by fixed and permanent laws, from the rage of the populace on one side, and the tyranny of a despot on the other, the aristocracy will and must rule; that is a number of the wealthiest individuals, and the heads of great families:—The perfection of all political wisdom is so to temper this aristocracy as to prevent oppression.'' A [Maryland] Farmer's view both of the problem and the solution was much like Adams': ''The only remedy the ingenuity of man has discovered for this evil is—a *properly constituted and independent executive,* a vindex injuriarum—an avenger of public wrongs; who with the assistance of a third estate, may enforce the rigor of equal law on those who are otherwise above the fear of punishment. . . .''[25] The result was of course a much less unfavorable view of a strong executive and even of hereditary orders than might have been expected.

Many Anti-Federalists shared something of this view, though few had A [Maryland] Farmer's insight. The Anti-Federal position is characterized, finally, not so much by a commitment to simple government as by a strong tendency to think in terms of a great and traditional alternative: on the one hand, simple, responsible government based on a small homogeneous population, and on the other hand, complex, balanced government based on more or less fixed and permanent orders. The Anti-Federalists were likely to hold that simple (or relatively simple) government is more conducive to freedom, that it should be preserved as long as possible, and that a hasty and crude attempt to imitate more mature forms can only be disastrous;[26] but many saw merit in a balance of orders, as well as a more or less irresistible tendency in that direction. Their argument was that the Constitution failed to provide adequately for *either* simple government *or* balanced government. It was an imitation of the British government, built without the essential British materials.

''In the British Government there are real balances and checks,'' Patrick Henry argued; ''In this system, there are only ideal balances. . . . The President and Senators have nothing to lose. They have not that interest in the preservation of the Government, that the King and Lords have in England. They will therefore be regardless of the interests of the people.'' This absence of checks based on the interests of permanent orders was what Henry meant when he said, ''tell me not of checks on paper, but tell me of checks founded on self-love.''*[27] Henry, who had earlier objected that the Constitution had a squint toward monarchy, was teased for his warm praise of the British monarchy; but he freely owned ''that if you cannot love a Republican Government, you may love the British monarchy. . . .''[28] In America there could be no genuine monarchy; nor were there the social materials for a genuine differentiation of the two branches of the legislature. Thus The Federal Farmer warned that ''the partitions between the two branches will be merely those of the building in which they sit: there will not be found in them any of those genuine balances and checks, among the real different interests, and efforts of the several classes of men in the community we aim at; nor can any such balances and checks be formed in the present condition of the United States in any considerable degree of perfection. . . ." The Federal Farmer thought that it was impossible that a Senate organized on "pure principles" could offset the democratic House of Representatives, and this important explanation followed:

I say, on pure principles; because I make a distinction between a senate that derives its weight and influence from a pure source, its numbers and wisdom, its extensive property, its extensive and permanent connections; and a senate composed of a few men, possessing small property, small and unstable connections, that derives its weight and influence from a corrupt or pernicious source; that is, merely from the power given it by the constitution and laws, to dispose of the public offices, and the annexed emoluments, and by those means to interest officers, and the hungry expectants of offices, in support of its measures. I wish the proposed senate may not partake too much of the latter description.*[29]

The Anti-Federalists were, here again, the conservatives, believing that the framers of the Constitution had fallen awkwardly and dangerously between the two stools of simple, responsible government and genuine balanced government. On the other hand, the Federalists claimed—or the most thoughtful of them did—that they had provided a new and better kind of balanced government. Consider, in contrast to The Federal Farmer's view of a senate, James Madison's proposal to his fellow delegates in Philadelphia. Madison argued that under American conditions the weight of the Senate would depend largely on the organization and powers given to it by the Constitution and not on anything intrinsic to its members or their social status. He urged the framers, that is to say, *not* to try to represent a certain social order or to represent property in the Senate (although neither of these is entirely absent, even in Madison's view), but to give their attention primarily to the constitutional organization, powers, and operation of the body, which would determine its weight and character and thus its part in the overall balance of the government.*[30] The Constitution established neither a simple government nor a traditional mixture of orders or estates. Neither was it an attempt, following John Adams and favored (once simple government was admitted to be impracticable) by many Anti-Federalists, to represent and balance the natural orders that exist in any civilized community. It was something new, at least in the sense that it was a full working out of principles partially or incompletely expressed in the state constitutions and in earlier American thinking.*[31] James Monroe saw the distinction clearly and, unlike many of his Anti-Federal colleagues, accepted the new view. In former governments, he explained, the object of the distribution of powers had been to maintain "a composition or mixture of aristocracy, democracy, and monarchy, each of which had a repellent quality which enabled it to preserve itself from being destroyed by the other two; so that the balance was continually maintained." In America, on the other hand, the object of the division of power is to provide "a more faithful and regular administration," and to prevent a union of governmental power, with all its dangers for the people.*[32] It is this new kind of balanced government that is described and defended in *The Federalist* and of which James Madison is the chief theoretician.

This new kind of balanced government can best be explored by approaching it through the separation of powers, the need for which, as Cecelia Kenyon correctly says, the Anti-Federalists fully accepted. A Pennsylvania Anti-Federalist made a common complaint when he wrote of the proposed Constitution that "the LEGISLATIVE and EXECUTIVE powers are not kept separate as every one of the American constitutions declares they ought to be; but they are mixed in a manner entirely novel and unknown, even in the constitution of Great Britain. . . ."[33] Even Centinel, who advocated a unicameral legislature, assumed as a matter of course "separating the executive and judicial." He argued, indeed, that "the chief improvement in government, in modern times, has been the compleat separation of the great distinctions of power; placing the *legislative* in different hands from those which held the *executive;* and again severing the *judicial* part from ordinary *administrative*." And Brutus, while contending for the principle of strict accountability to the people, went on to say that "to have a government well administered in all its parts, it is requisite the different departments of it should be separated and lodged as much as may be in different hands."[34]

The assumption behind such a separation (although neither Federalists nor Anti-Federalists give it much attention) is that all governments perform certain kinds of functions, which are best performed in distinctive ways and by distinctive kinds of bodies. "It is one of the greatest advantages of a government of different branches, that each branch may be conveniently made conformable to the nature of the business assigned to it. . . ."*[35] The legislative function requires large numbers, more or less public gatherings, procedures to foster deliberation, etc. The executive function requires, as was said so often, secrecy, energy and dispatch. Judging requires manifest impartiality and special training in the artificial reasoning of the law. With each branch distinct from the others, each can perform its function in its appropriate way. This division is not aimed primarily at mutual checking but at the efficient performance of certain kinds of tasks.*[36] But two considerations of mutual checking immediately enter. First, there is a political dividend arising out of the functional distinction and the independence of the several branches: if one department becomes tyrannical or stupid, the others may remain sound and thus, to some extent, prevent tyranny or stupidity from seizing the whole government. Second, however, the functional distinction needs to be secured. To maintain their distinctiveness the different branches must be independent, and they require some defense of their independence. Mere parchment barriers will not suffice. Each branch will tend to encroach on the others, if only because of the extreme difficulty of drawing perfectly clear lines between their respective functions. "After discriminating, therefore, in theory, the several classes of power, as they may in their nature be legislative, executive, or judiciary, the next and most difficult task is to provide some practical security for each, against the invasion of the others."[37] There are two ways of doing this: by providing an appeal to some common superior—in this case presumably the people themselves—or by providing a capacity of self-defense in the several branches. The former, apart from its other difficulties, is scarcely feasible for everyday use in a large and diverse country, and it was not in fact advocated as such by the Anti-Federalists.*[38] The latter was the main reliance in the Constitution, as it had been in Britain and in the states. This required that the three branches be brought into legitimate contact with one another to avoid illegitimate encroachment; they must be brought together for the purpose of keeping them apart.[39] Thus the executive might be given a veto over legislation for the purpose of securing executive independence, which is in turn necessary to perform effectively the executive function. Most of the Anti-Federalists accepted this in principle,*[40] although some seemed to think that even this limited "mixing" should be avoided, and many thought that the Constitution had gone so far in the mixing as to endanger the separation. While it is true that there may be an incidental security deriving from such checks, the emphasis intended is on the functional discrimination.

Another step in this argument is to regard separation as a way of promoting wise deliberation. Thus one Federalist writer denied Centinel's contention that the branches "were intended to balance one another," explaining that "they all have the same interest"—i.e., that they do not represent different estates or orders.*[41] "The sole intention of [the separation] is to produce wise and mature deliberation. Experience teaches us that individuals or simple bodies of men are liable to rash and hasty decisions—to party influence and cabal—that we are generally fond of what originates with ourselves—and that another person of no greater ability than ourselves, will easily discern a blemish in our productions to which we are blind until it be pointed out."*[42] Arguments like this were extensions of the view of the separation of powers as promoting the proper conduct of the government's business by keeping the bodies that perform the functions of government separate and distinct.

In practice it is easy to move from considerations of this kind to a different notion of "balanced government," in which the separation of governmental power and mutual checking are seen as desirable quite apart from functional differentiation. In principle, however, this second view originates not with different governmental functions and their different modes but with government or political power per se. Political power is necessary but it is dangerous, and a way of guarding against the danger is to divide the power and arrange it in ways that prevent too much of it from accumulating in any one set of hands. Since the sovereign power in a state was traditionally held to reside in the legislature, the problem of concentration of power and the solution of dividing and balancing power were often applied to the legislature only.*[43] There is no necessary identity between this separation of *power,* as we may call it, and the earlier separation of *functions.* A usual view would have been that there should be a separation of the legislative, executive, and judicial *functions* and a separation and balancing of *power* within the legislature. (And this would be likely, in turn, to be connected, as in Adams' case, with the balancing of social orders.) However, a separation of functions and a separation of power easily become linked and confused. The functional differentiation can be used to distribute power.*[44] In particular, the legislature may not only be divided from within but it may be made part of a broader balance. The practical danger of legislative sovereignty is met by external as well as internal checks. And the theoretical claim of legislative sovereignty is met by the notion that the legislature is not sovereign but is the mere creature of the Constitution (behind which stands of course the people), which apportions power to the legislature and establishes limits on it as one among several instrumentalities of government and which enforces those limits by a nicely arranged scheme of constitutional (not merely legislative) balance.

The complex or balanced government provided for in the Constitution is, then, fundamentally a balance of *constitutional* orders or powers, blended with a constitutional differentiation of functions, formed by the makers of the Constitution and requiring only the impulse of popular consent to breathe life into it and the private interests and ambitions of citizens and representatives to keep it in motion. It was on this basis that James Wilson considered it the distinction of the Americans to have invented a mixed government made wholly out of popular elements. "What is the nature and kind of that government which has been proposed for the United States by the late Convention? In its principle, it is purely democratical. But that principle is applied in different forms, in order to obtain the advantages, and exclude the inconveniences, of the simple modes of government."*[45] The differences are not derived from natural or conventional differentiations of society but are constitutional or legal constructs.

In their different ways and according to their various capacities, the Anti-Federalists doubted the theoretical soundness, the practical feasibility, and even the good intentions of this new kind of balanced government.*[46] While accepting the need for a separation of functions—and typically insisting that the Constitution did not go far enough in this respect—the Anti-Federalists became uneasy as concern shifted to what we have called a separation and balancing of power. They conceded only reluctantly the insufficiency of simple popular government, and they were likely to judge constitutional arrangements according to how well they secured popular responsibility, a test that the proposed Constitution seemed to fail. Moreover, to the extent that the Anti-Federalists accepted the need for some form of complex government beyond a mere division of functions, they thought in traditional terms of a government composed of representatives of social orders—either the fixed orders of a mature Britain or the natural orders of a youthful America. Only such a mixture, intimately tied to the divisions inherent in society, could provide genuine checks among the parts of the government and thereby prevent the government from becoming independent of and hostile to the society. The Anti-Federalists admitted that there were slender materials for such a mixture in the United States, which was all the more reason for proceeding slowly and letting American government mature as American society matured. Instead, the framers rushed into a mere constitutional imitation of mixed government, which combined great powers with severely limited popular responsibility and ineffective internal checks.

8
Bill of Rights

It is often said that the major legacy of the Anti-Federalists is the Bill of Rights. Many of their suggestions found their way into the proposals for amendment made by state ratifying conventions and thence into the first ten amendments adopted in 1791. Three kinds of rights were stressed: the usual common law procedural rights in criminal prosecutions, liberty of conscience, and liberty of the press. The Anti-Federalists insisted that the Constitution should explicitly recognize the traditional procedural rights: to be safe from general search and seizure, to be indicted by grand jury, to trial by jury, to confront witnesses, and to be protected against cruel and unusual punishments. The most important of these was the trial by jury, and one of the most widely uttered objections against the Constitution was that it did not provide for (and therefore effectively abolished) trial by jury in civil cases. The Federalists' claim that practice among the states in this respect varied too much to provide a general rule was either denied by the Anti-Federalists or used as a further argument against the feasibility of consolidation. Regarding liberty of conscience, the Anti-Federalists' position was complex. Typically they favored both governmental encouragement of religion and liberty of individual conscience.[1] The first proposal of the minority of the Pennsylvania convention was that rights of conscience shall be held inviolable and that no state provision regarding liberty of conscience shall be abridged by the federal government.*[2] Some Anti-Federalists professed to see in the prohibition against a religious test for officers of the United States a power to regulate religious beliefs in general, to which this prohibition was an exception.*[3] The rights of conscience should be secured, even though there was no immediate threat. Times change, and "the seeds of superstition, bigotry and enthusiasm, are too deeply implanted in our minds, ever to be eradicated. . . ."[4] The third area of concern was liberty of the press, often declaimed upon by the Anti-Federalists as the palladium of American liberties.*[5] "It is the opinion of some great writers," Centinel argued, "that if the liberty of the press, by an institution of religion, or otherwise, could be rendered sacred, even in *Turkey,* that despotism would fly before it." "I say," another Anti-Federalist insisted, "that a declaration of those inherent and political rights ought to be made in a BILL OF RIGHTS, that the people may never lose their liberties by construction. If the liberty of the press be an inherent political right, let it be so declared, that no despot however great shall *dare to gain say it*.''*⁶ All of these concerns were pressed with enough vigor so that the Constitution was adopted only on the understanding that one of the first items of business of the new government would be the framing of amendments.

While the Federalists gave us the Constitution, then, the legacy of the Anti-Federalists was the Bill of Rights. But it is an ambiguous legacy, as can be seen by studying the debate. Indeed, in one sense, the success of the Bill of Rights reflects the failure of the Anti-Federalists. The whole emphasis on reservations of rights of individuals implied a fundamental acceptance of the ''consolidated'' character of the new government. A truly federal government needs no bill of rights. Indeed, there were some Federalists who tried to use the Anti-Federalists' federalism to destroy the Anti-Federalists' argument for a bill of rights (incidentally undermining their own position). One Alfredus contended, for example, that a bill of rights was not necessary because the Constitution was a compact not between individuals but between sovereign and independent societies.⁷ This argument is easy enough to answer, and the Anti-Federalists often answered it: the government under the Constitution was not a mere compact of sovereign states—at least not in its operation—and it was not exempt from the need for a bill of rights on that account. But in making this reply the Anti-Federalists decisively abandoned the doctrine of strict federalism.

A more substantial ''federal'' argument against a bill of rights was made by James Wilson in his famous ''State house speech'' of 4 October 1787. Wilson acknowledged the maxim often put forward by the Anti-Federalists that in establishing governments all powers not expressly reserved are presumed to be granted, but he denied that it applied to the proposed general government, because that was to be a government of specifically enumerated powers. Whereas in the state constitutions the people ''invested their representatives with every right and authority which they did not in explicit terms reserve,'' under the proposed Constitution ''the congressional power is to be collected, not from tacit implication, but from the positive grant expressed in the instrument of the union. Hence, it is evident, that in the former case, everything which is not reserved is given; but in the latter the reverse of the proposition prevails, and everything which is not given is reserved.'' Thus, Wilson concluded, ''it would have been superfluous and absurd to have stipulated with a federal body of our own creation, that we should enjoy those privileges of which we are not divested, either by the intention or the act that has brought the body into existence.''⁸ This is a substantial argument; it was heavily relied on by defenders of the Constitution; and the basic theory on which it rests has become a part of American constitutional orthodoxy. Yet it has some serious difficulties, especially when applied to the question of a bill of rights.

Wilson's position depends on the assumption that the ''powers'' delegated to the government are fairly easily identifiable and unambiguous.

Thus, for example, he contended that there is no "power" granted to the federal government "to regulate literary publications" and therefore no need for a reservation in favor of liberty of the press. If Congress should enact such a law, the judges would declare it null and void because "inconsistent with those powers vested by this instrument in Congress. . . ."[9] But (even leaving aside the question of libel and seditious libel)[10] the general government is given authority to lay and collect taxes and to regulate commerce, for example, and could not either of these be used to stifle the press? More generally, does not the general government, in the pursuit of its delegated powers, have implied powers that need to be limited for the sake of individual liberties? Cannot the federal government define crimes and criminal procedures, in connection with federal postal regulations, for example; and is there not therefore a need for procedural restraints of the traditional kind? Brutus made the argument thus: "The powers, rights, and authority, granted to the general government by this constitution, are as complete, with respect to every object to which they extend, as that of any state government—It reaches to every thing which concerns human happiness—Life, liberty, and property, are under its controul. There is the same reason, therefore, that the exercise of power, in this case, should be restrained within proper limits, as in that of the state governments."[11]

The constitutional grant of power to Congress—so laconic and broad—is an argument in favor of a bill of rights, not against it. In fact, said the satirical Aristocrotis, "this constitution is much better and gives more scope to the rulers than they durst safely take if there was no constitution at all; for then the people might contend that the power was inherent in them; and that they had made some implied reserves in the original grant; but now they cannot, for every thing is expressly given away to government in this plan."[12] Who can overrule the pretensions of Congress that any particular law is "necessary and proper"? "No one; unless we had a bill of rights to which we might appeal, and under which we might contend against any assumption of undue power and appeal to the judicial branch of the government to protect us by their judgements."[13]

The inadequacy of Wilson's argument is further demonstrated by the presence in the Constitution of a truncated bill of rights. Why was there any need to restrict the suspension of the writ of habeas corpus or to prohibit granting titles of nobility? Where were such powers granted? The very few Federalists who made any attempt to meet this objection sought to show that these were exceptions to implied powers,[14] but this only reenforced the contention that the "powers" granted are anything but simple and unambiguous—that they are in fact complex and doubtful and capable of great extension.

Nor was it any use to point, as some Federalists did, to the state bills of rights or to the general principles of the common law. The Constitution is an original compact, dependent on nothing but itself. It "is not dependent on any other book for an explanation, and contains no reference to any other book. All the defences of it, therefore, so far as they are drawn from the state constitutions, or from maxims of the common law, are foreign to the purpose."[15]

Even if it were granted that a bill of rights was, strictly speaking, unnecessary, the Anti-Federalists asked, why not be safe? What is the harm? Would it, Patrick Henry asked, have taken too much paper? One answer was that a bill of rights would be positively dangerous, because, as Wilson explained, "it would imply that whatever is not expressed was given, which is not the principle of the proposed constitution."[16] There is some basis for this view. Yet the Anti-Federalists could forcefully contend that any harm of this kind had already been done by the reservations in behalf of individual rights included in the Constitution. And, all things considered, this Federalist argument seemed a bit sophistical. "This indeed is a distinction of which the votaries of scholastic philosophy might be proud—but in the political world, where reason is not cultivated independently of action and experience, such futile distinctions ought not to be agitated."[17]

Despite all their rhetorical emphasis on a bill of rights, however, the Anti-Federalists were typically quite doubtful about the practical utility of this kind of provision in the new Constitution. Thus Samuel Chase wrote to John Lamb, "A declaration of rights alone will be of no essential service. Some of the powers must be abridged, or public liberties will be endangered, and, in time, destroyed."[18] Of far more practical importance than bills of rights were the powers and structure of the general government—the unlimited power to tax, for example, and the inadequate representation in the federal legislature. A bill of rights, without more, would make little difference. Why, then, did the Anti-Federalists emphasize a bill of rights as much as they did? Why did they invite the brilliantly successful Federalist tactic of first standing fast on all points, then opening the door to a bill of rights and watching the Anti-Federalists stumble through it to a strong national government? In some cases they doubted that they could win on the greater questions. In many cases they must have been influenced by the rhetorical attractiveness of arguments for bills of rights compared to arguments about state prerogatives and federal powers. But there were also deeper reasons. The debate over the bill of rights was an extension of the general debate over the nature of limited government, and at this level the Anti-Federalists can perhaps claim a substantial, though not unmitigated, accomplishment.

"I presume," one Anti-Federalist wrote, "that the liberty of a nation depends, not on planning the frame of government, which consists merely in fixing and delineating the powers thereof; but on prescribing due limits to those powers, and establishing them upon just principles."[19] Yet this seems a bit odd. If liberty depends on establishing *limits* on government, what is government itself for? The problem arises even more sharply in a comment by the wise Brutus: " . . . in forming a government on its true principles, the foundation should be laid . . . by expressly reserving to the people such of their essential natural rights, as are not necessary to be parted with."[20] Again, is this not putting the cart before the horse? However necessary a reservation of rights may be, how can the *foundation* of government be laid in *reservations* against that very government? To answer that question is to grasp the Anti-Federalist case for a bill of rights in its most fundamental aspect.

The Federalists contended that the proponents of a bill of rights failed to grasp the crucial fact that a constitution *is* a bill of rights. A bill of rights was unnecessary, Judge McKean told the Pennsylvania ratifying convention; "for in fact the whole plan of government is nothing more than a bill of rights—a declaration of the people in what manner they choose to be governed."[21] "What have we to do with bills of rights?" Edmund Randolph asked his fellow Virginians. Many states have none, and the predilection for it has arisen from a misunderstanding of its principles. In England, where the king might do what he liked in the absence of restraint, the bill of rights is needed; but in a republic it is useless if not dangerous.[22] A country free from its birth and resting on constitutions establishing government and granting its powers has no need to imitate the bills of rights of a country that established its liberty by gradual encroachments on royal prerogative.[23] The place to look for security of liberty is not in bills of rights, Benjamin Rush said, but in a pure and adequate representation. He considered it "an honor to the late convention, that this system has not been disgraced with a bill of rights," although he intended no reflection upon those states "which have encumbered their constitutions with that idle and superfluous instrument."[24] "Men in full possession and enjoyment of all their natural rights, cannot lose them but in two ways, either from their own consent, or from tyranny. This Constitution, neither implies the former, nor creates an avenue to the latter. Therefore no cause can operate to this effect,—because the *people,* are always both able and ready, to resist the encroachments of Supreme Power."[25]

One reply to these arguments—one that strikes the Federalists close to home—is that the supremacy of the people does not secure the rights of individuals and minorities against the majority. As we have seen, some of the Anti-Federalists argued that one of the functions of a bill of rights in a republican government is to serve as a check against majority faction. To the question, whom does a bill of rights protect in a popular government? Agrippa answered: "such a government is indeed a government by ourselves; but as a just government protects all alike, it is necessary that the sober and industrious part of the community should be defended from the rapacity and violence of the vicious and idle. A bill of rights therefore ought to set forth the purposes for which the compact is made, and serves to secure the minority against the usurpation and tyranny of the majority."[26]

Moreover, the Anti-Federalists contended that *this* constitution was not an adequate bill of rights. If ever there was a case for an explicit reservation of individual rights, the proposed constitution provided one, with its very extensive powers, its shadow of genuine representation, and its weak and dubious checks on the encroachments of the few. Identical considerations apply to the Federalist argument that the states would serve as powerful checks on the general government.[27] If the general government lays excessive taxes, "the constitution will provide . . . no remedy for the people or the states—the people must bear them, or have recourse, not to any constitutional checks or remedies, but to that resistance which is the last resort, and founded in self-defence."[*28] The state legislatures can only check the general legislators "by exciting the people to resist constitutional laws."[*29] The best of the Federalists understood the validity of this point. Although they judged the states' intrinsic advantages to be weightier, longer-lasting, and more dangerous than did the Anti-Federalists, they saw that the Constitution placed the weight of legality on the side of the federal government. The ultimate check is, indeed, the revolutionary one, made more significant, however, by the support and coherence that the state governments will lend the populace in case of such an ultimate resort. After all, Publius emphasized, along with many defenders of the Constitution, the ultimate security of the people rests in their understanding of their rights and their willingness to defend them.[*30]

This leads to the deepest level of the argument over a bill of rights. The final Federalist answer to the question, what harm can a bill of rights do? was the seldom explicitly stated fear that a bill of rights, especially undue emphasis on a bill of rights, might weaken *government,* which is the first protection of rights and which was in 1787 in particular need of strengthening. The first defense of individual rights is a government able to accomplish the necessary tasks of self-defense, regulation of commerce, administration of justice, etc. Loose and easy talk about rights was likely to distract attention from the difficult but fundamental business of forming a government capable of doing the things that have to be done to protect rights.[*31]

The Anti-Federalists replied that the need for government is not yet the bedrock of the free republic. For there remains the question, what does that government depend on? On nothing, as the Federalists themselves admit, but the people themselves, specifically on the people's understanding of the purpose of government, their sharp-eyed scrutiny of the actions of government, and their willingness to resist the encroachments of that government on their own behalf and that of their fellow citizens. An enumeration of individual rights and of the basic principles of free government at the head of the Constitution "can inspire and conserve the affection of the native country, they will be the first lesson of the young citizens becoming men, to sustain the dignity of their being. . . ." Specific reservations in favor of individual liberty actually strengthen republican government by strengthening the people's attachment to it.[32] Even admitting that all rights not expressly given up are reserved, and admitting of course that no bill of rights can add anything to men's natural rights, there are "infinite advantages," The Federal Farmer insisted, in an enumeration of reserved rights.

We do not by declarations change the nature of things, or create new truths, but we give existence, or at least establish in the minds of the people truths and principles which they might never otherwise have thought of, or soon forgot. If a nation means its systems, religious or political, shall have duration, it ought to recognize the leading principles of them in the front page of every family book.[33]

This is the reason for bills of rights serving, as they often did in the state constitutions, as *preambles,* often of an exhortatory kind. This is the reason for apparently paradoxical arguments like that of Brutus, that reservations of individual rights precede, in principle, the very government against which those reservations are made. The fundamental case for a bill of rights is that it can be a prime agency of that political and moral education of the people on which free republican government depends. The famous Virginia Declaration of Rights of 1776 held "that no free government, or the blessings of liberty, can be preserved to any people, but by a firm adherence to justice, moderation, temperance, frugality, and virtue, and by frequent recurrence to fundamental principles."[34] One of the main texts in which these principles are to be read is a well-formed bill of rights, reminding citizens of the beginning and therefore of the end of civil government.

9

Conclusion

The Anti-Federalists lost the debate over the Constitution not merely because they were less clever arguers or less skillful politicians but because
they had the weaker argument. They were, as Publius said, trying to reconcile contradictions. There was no possibility of instituting the small republic in the United States, and the Anti-Federalists themselves were not
willing to pay the price that such an attempt would have required. A basis
for republican government and the solution of the problems of republican
government had somehow to be found in the great and complex republic. To
this task the framers directed their attention, and the Constitution was their
magnificent response. The Federalists, moreover, reminded Americans that
the true principle of the Revolution was not hostility to government but
hostility to tyrannical government. They sought to recover the balance that
Americans had lost in the zeal of revolution. "There is no quarrel between
government and liberty; the former is the shield and protector of the latter.
The war is between government and licentiousness, faction, turbulence, and
other violations of the rules of society, to preserve liberty."[1]

In the commencement of a revolution which received its birth from the
usurpations of tyranny, nothing was more natural than that the public mind
should be influenced by an extreme spirit of jealousy. To resist these encroachments, and to nourish this spirit, was the great object of all our public
and private institutions. The zeal for liberty became predominant and excessive. In forming our Confederation, this passion alone seemed to actuate
us, and we appear to have had no other view than to secure ourselves from
despotism. The object certainly was a valuable one, and deserved our utmost attention; but, sir, there is another object, equally important, and
which our enthusiasm rendered us little capable of regarding: I mean a
principle of *strength* and *stability* in the organization of our government, and
vigor in its operations.*[2]

The framers of the Articles of Confederation, misled by the vigor and
good sense displayed by the people during the war, made the "amiable
mistake" of thinking that the Americans needed no government, "that the
people of America only required to know what ought to be done to do it."[3]
The Americans are, however, like other men, which is to say that they
cannot be relied on to govern themselves voluntarily. The Anti-Federalists'
fondness for the small republic and their concern with the inculcation of
civic virtue amounted to an attempt to push aside this harsh truth.[4] Thus

they refused to accept, or they accepted only halfheartedly, that the prime need was a government with a capacity to govern and not dependent for its goodness and trustworthiness on the everyday goodness and trustworthiness of the people or their representatives. The Constitution was designed so that, as far as possible, the ordinary operations of government would call for little more than the reliable inclination of men to follow their own interests, fairly narrowly understood. This system has been remarkably, if not gloriously, successful.

If, however, the foundation of the American polity was laid by the Federalists, the Anti-Federalist reservations echo through American history; and it is in the dialogue, not merely in the Federalist victory, that the country's principles are to be discovered. The Anti-Federalists were easily able to show that the Constitution did not escape reliance on republican virtue. One of the chief replies to the critics' descriptions of dangers of the new and powerful general government was that the American people could be trusted to elect good men to office and to keep them under scrutiny while there. There were frequent remarks like that of James Wilson that the framers must have assumed that the people and the states would give proper attention to the men elected to the legislature: "If they should now do otherwise, the fault will not be in Congress, but in the people . . . themselves. I have mentioned oftener than once, that for a people wanting to themselves, there is no remedy."[5] "Let the Americans be virtuous," an anonymous Federalist wrote, "let them be firm supporters of Republicanism—let them have confidence in their representatives—then their Liberties will be secured to them, and peace and prosperity will ensue."*[6] Nor were these only the arguments of lesser Federalist thinkers or the ones least free of the old reliance on civic virtue. Madison himself defended the provisions for representation on the ground that "the people will have virtue and intelligence to select men of virtue and wisdom." He went on to ask:

Is there no virtue among us? If there be not, we are in a wretched situation. No theoretical checks, no form of government, can render us secure. To suppose that any form of government will secure liberty or happiness without any virtue in the people is a chimerical idea. If there be sufficient virtue and intelligence in the community, it will be exercised in the selection of these men; so that we do not depend on their virtue, or put confidence in our rulers, but in the people who are to choose them.[7]

Publius, too, perhaps the least equivocal advocate of the constitutional system of channeled self-interest, remarked that the genius of the American people is such as to make it unlikely that they will put up with the loss of their liberty, or will take no interest in the activities of the government, or will choose ignorant or bad men as representatives. The crucial point is conceded in *The Federalist,* no. 55, where Publius argues that "as there is a degree of depravity in mankind which requires a certain degree of circumspection and distrust, so there are other qualities in human nature, which justify a certain portion of esteem and confidence. Republican government presupposes the existence of these qualities in a higher degree than any other form."[8] Publius did not here name the "other qualities"—itself a point of some interest—but they must include an enlightened understanding of the objects of government, a degree of public-spiritedness, a participation in citizenship as distinct from a merely private life.

Given this kind of argument, the Anti-Federalists could rightly contend that the new Constitution does, after all, depend on something like republican virtue. It is distinguished not by emancipation from this old dependence but by a lack of much attention to the question of how that necessary republican virtue can be maintained. As they took for granted a certain kind of public-spirited leadership,*[9] so they took for granted the republican genius of the people; but that cannot prudently be taken for granted.

The Federalist solution not only failed to provide for the moral qualities that are necessary to the maintenance of republican government; it tended to undermine them. Will not the constitutional regime, the Anti-Federalists asked, with its emphasis on private, self-seeking, commercial activities, release and foster a certain type of human being who will be likely to destroy that very regime?

It is alledged that the opinions and manners of the people of America, are capable to resist and prevent an extension of prerogative or oppression; but you must recollect that opinion and manners are mutable, and may not always be a permanent obstruction against the encroachments of government; that the progress of a commercial society begets luxury, the parent of inequality, the foe to virtue, and the enemy to restraint; and that ambition and voluptuousness aided by flattery, will teach magistrates, where limits are not explicitly fixed to have separate and distinct interests from the people, besides it will not be denied that government assimilates the manners and opinions of the community to it. Therefore, a general presumption that rulers will govern well is not a sufficient security.*[10]

Can a legal system for the regulation of private passions to the end that those passions may be more fully gratified serve as the foundation of civic virtue? Montesquieu argued that the virtue required in a republican government is "the love of laws and of our country," that such love "requires a constant preference of public to private interest," that "every thing . . . depends on establishing this love in a republic; and to inspire it ought to be the principal business of education. . . ."[11] The question is whether the Constitution, as the Federalists understood it, succeeded in laying that argument to rest. The Anti-Federalists contended that it did not; "Whatever the refinement of modern politics may inculcate, it still is certain that some degree of virtue must exist, or freedom cannot live." They rejected "Mandervill's [sic] position . . . 'that private vices are public benefits.' . . ."[12]

The Federalists did not, it should be emphasized, rely on some unseen hand to produce public good out of individual selfishness. The foundation was the Constitution, and the working of the system depended upon an attachment of the people to the Constitution. It was admitted that that attachment was not sufficiently assured by narrow self-interest. Whereas the Federalists regarded this as a somewhat peripheral problem, however, to be dealt with by avoiding certain kinds of mistakes and providing auxiliary institutions, such as judicial review, the Anti-Federalists saw it as a permanent and central concern of the republic.

The matter was canvassed most profoundly on the Federalist side by Publius in *The Federalist,* no. 49, and by Chief Justice John Marshall in his Opinion in *Marbury* v. *Madison.*[13] A brief consideration of the former will suffice for the present purpose. The specific question was how to settle disputes between the different departments of government and whether provision should be made, as Jefferson had suggested, for appeals in such cases to the people. Publius treated this proposal with great respect, due not only to its author but also to its theoretical cogency, given the principles of popular government; but he rejected it. Two arguments are of special importance here. First, he suggested that every appeal to the people "would carry an implication of some defect in the government," and "frequent appeals would in great measure deprive the government of that veneration, which time bestows on every thing, and without which perhaps the wisest and freest governments would not possess the requisite stability." While a nation of philosophers would be led to revere the laws by an enlightened reason, "in every other nation, the most rational government will not find it a superfluous advantage, to have the prejudices of the community on its side." Second, Publius pointed to the danger of "disturbing the public tranquillity by interesting too strongly the public passions. . . . Notwithstanding the success which has attended the revisions of our established forms of government and which does so much honor to the virtue and intelligence of the people of America, it must be confessed that the experiments are of too ticklish a nature to be unnecessarily multiplied."*[14]

The basis of this argument is a radical disjunction between the founding of the government and its operation. The circumstances conducive to the good operation of a government under a properly constructed constitution (e.g., a wide variety of interests) are extremely pernicious in the making or altering of the Constitution.[15] American constitutional reform occurred during a time when sharp diversities of opinion were muted and patriotic sentiments relatively great, when confidence in leaders was high, and when excesses of liberty had made the people willing to accept a sound constitution. It was the Americans' good fortune that the need for constitutional reform coincided with circumstances conducive to it, but these circumstances are rare and the coincidence unlikely. As a general rule, "a people does not reform with moderation."[16] It is necessary that every precaution be taken not to upset that original patriotic act and to preserve and foster reverence for the laws, and particularly for the highest law. The Federalist authors did not argue, as Lincoln later did, that reverence for the laws ought to become the political religion of the nation. They took a narrower view of the problem and proposed more modest means. The task of basic lawmaking having been done, in the main successfully, the aim must be to avoid reopening the fundamental political questions, which were hardly likely to be so well answered another time, and to let time do its work of fostering veneration. Publius' argument was a negative one: do nothing to disturb "that veneration, which time bestows on everything."

But will the mere passage of time be enough? Many of the Anti-Federalists thought that it would not, that the passage of time would magnify the difficulty of preserving the American republic, rather than overcoming it. The Revolutionary preoccupation with liberty, which may have made men forget the need for government, nevertheless had a profound effect in holding the American governments true to their ends. And the spirit of the Revolution was a spirit of dedication to the common good.

It is next to impossible to enslave a people immediately after a firm struggle against oppression, while the sense of past injury is recent and strong. But after some time this impression naturally wears off;—the ardent glow of freedom gradually evaporates;—the charms of popular equality, which arose from the *republican plan*, insensibly decline;—the pleasures, the advantages derived from the new kind of government grow stale through use. Such declension in all those vigorous springs of action necessarily produces a supineness. The altar of liberty is no longer watched with such attentive assiduity;—a new train of passions succeeds to the empire of the mind;—different objects of desire take place;—and, if the nation happens to enjoy a series of prosperity, voluptuousness, excessive fondness for riches, and luxury gain admission and establish themselves—these produce venality and corruption of every kind, which open a fatal avenue to bribery. Hence it follows, that in the midst of this general contageon a few men—or one—more powerful than all the others, industriously endeavor to obtain all authority; and by means of great wealth—or embezzling the public money,—perhaps totally subvert the government, and erect a system of aristocratical or monarchic tyranny in its room. . . . It is this depravation of manners, this wicked propensity, my dear countrymen, against which you ought to provide with the utmost degree of prudence and circumspection. All nations pass this *parokism* of vice at some period or other;—and if at that dangerous juncture your government is not secure upon a solid foundation, and well guarded against the machinations of evil men, the liberties of this country will be lost—perhaps forever!*[17]

This view is strikingly like that of Abraham Lincoln in his speech in 1838 on "The Perpetuation of Our Political Institutions."[18] And some of the Anti-Federalists also saw the need, if the country was to survive its great moral crises, of leaders "who have genius and capacity sufficient to form the manners and correct the morals of the people, and virtue enough to lead their country to freedom."[19]

Indeed, the crisis might not be so far off. The post-Revolutionary period was a time, Federalists and Anti-Federalists seem to have agreed, when

75

men's lives, thoughts, and guiding principles were increasingly detached from the community. The Anti-Federalists thought that the Constitution would strengthen this tendency, and they feared for the Republic. It is a simplification, but not a misleading simplification, to say that the crisis faced by Abraham Lincoln seventy years later required a synthesis of the Federalist solution and the Anti-Federalist reservation. And if the major element in the synthesis was still the Federal one, yet it is due the Anti-Federalists to say that it was they, more than the defenders of the Constitution, who anticipated the need. The Anti-Federalists saw, although sometimes only dimly, the insufficiency of a community of mere interest.*[20] They saw that the American polity had to be a moral community if it was to be anything, and they saw that the seat of that community must be the hearts of the people.

Mercy Warren's reflections a decade after the adoption of the Constitution—not bitter or partisan reflections, but somewhat melancholy ones—suggest a question about the American experiment that is not less vital today than it was in the 1780s or the 1850s.

[S]uch a people as the Americans cannot suddenly be reduced to a state of slavery; it is a work of time to obliterate old opinions, founded in reason, and fanned by enthusiasm, till they had become a part of the religious creed of a nation. Notwithstanding the apprehensions which have pervaded the minds of many, America will probably long retain a greater share of freedom than can perhaps be found in any other part of the civilized world. This may be more the result of her local situation, than from her superior policy or moderation. From the general equality of fortune which had formerly reigned among them, it may be modestly asserted, that most of the inhabitants of America were too proud for monarchy, yet too poor for nobility, and it is to be feared, too selfish and avaricious for a virtuous republic.[21]

Works Frequently Cited

John Adams, *Works*	*The Works of John Adams,* ed. Charles Francis Adams (Boston 1851)
Cranch	Cranch's United States Supreme Court Reports, 1801–15
Crosskey, *Politics and the Constitution*	William W. Crosskey, *Politics and the Constitution in the History of the United States* (Chicago 1953)
Curtis, *Constitutional History*	George Ticknor Curtis, *Constitutional History of the United States: From Their Declaration of Independence to the Close of the Civil War* (New York 1889)
Dall.	Dallas' Pennsylvania and United States Reports, 1790–1800
Documentary History of the Constitution	*A Documentary History of the Constitution of the United States of America, 1786–1870; Derived from the Records, Manuscripts, and Rolls Deposited in the Bureau of Rolls and Library of the Department of State* (Washington, D.C., 1894–1905)
Elliot	*The Debates of the State Conventions on the Adoption of the Federal Constitution, as Recommended by the General Convention at Philadelphia in 1787,* 2d ed., ed. Jonathan Elliot (Philadelphia 1866)
Evans, *Early American Imprints*	Charles Evans, *Early American Imprints, 1639–1800* (Worcester, Mass., 1955–)
Farrand	*The Records of the Federal Convention of 1787,* ed. Max Farrand (New Haven 1911–37)
The Federalist	*The Federalist,* ed. Jacob E. Cooke (Middletown, Conn., 1961)
Ford, *Essays*	*Essays on the Constitution of the United States, Published during Its Discussion by the People, 1787–1788,* ed. Paul Leicester Ford (Brooklyn, N.Y., 1892)

Ford, *Pamphlets*	*Pamphlets on the Constitution of the United States, Published during Its Discussion by the People, 1787–1788,* ed. Paul Leicester Ford (Brooklyn, N.Y., 1888)
How.	Howard's United States Supreme Court Reports, 1843–60
Jensen, *New Nation*	Merrill Jensen, *The New Nation* (New York 1950)
Lee, *Letters*	*The Letters of Richard Henry Lee,* ed. James Curtis Ballagh (New York 1911–14)
Lincoln, *Collected Works*	Abraham Lincoln, *Collected Works,* ed. Roy P. Basler (New Brunswick, N.J., 1953)
Lincoln, *Speeches and Writings*	*Abraham Lincoln: His Speeches and Writings,* ed. Roy P. Basler (Cleveland and New York 1946)
Madison, *Writings* (ed. Hunt)	*The Writings of James Madison,* ed. Gaillard Hunt (New York 1900–1910)
Main, *Antifederalists*	Jackson Turner Main, *The Antifederalists: Critics of the Constitution* (Chapel Hill, N.C., 1960)
McMaster and Stone	*Pennsylvania and the Federal Constitution, 1787–1788,* ed. John Bach McMaster and Frederick D. Stone (Published for the Subscribers by the Historical Society of Pennsylvania, 1888)
Thorpe, *Federal and State Constitutions*	*The Federal and State Constitutions, Colonial Charters, and Other Organic Laws of the States, Territories, and Colonies Now or Heretofore Forming the United States of America,* comp. Francis Newton Thorpe (Washington, D.C., 1931–44)
Washington, *Writings*	*The Writings of George Washington from the Original Manuscript Sources, 1745–1799,* ed. John C. Fitzpatrick (Washington, D.C., 1931–44)
Wheat.	Wheaton's United States Supreme Court Reports, 1816–27
Wood, *Creation*	Gordon Wood, *The Creation of the American Republic, 1776–1787* (Chapel Hill, N.C., 1969)

Notes

An asterisk indicates a note of substance. References to *The Complete Anti-Federalist* (e.g., Martin 2.4.36) are by volume, position of an essay or series of essays in the volume, and paragraph. For contents, see below, pp. 101–6. For works cited in shortened form, see above, pp. 77–78.

CHAPTER ONE

1. See John Fiske, *The Critical Period of American History, 1783–1789* (Boston 1888) ch. 7; George Bancroft, *History of the Formation of the Constitution of the United States of America* (New York 1882) II, book 4 passim; George Ticknor Curtis, *Constitutional History of the United States: From Their Declaration of Independence to the Close of the Civil War* (New York 1889) I, 626; Andrew McLaughlin, *The Confederation and the Constitution, 1783–1789* (New York 1905) ch. 17; Forrest McDonald, *E Pluribus Unum* (Boston 1965) 208.

2. Charles A. Beard, *An Economic Interpretation of the Constitution* (New York 1913, 1935); Merrill Jensen, *The Articles of Confederation* (Madison, Wisc., 1940); Jensen, *The New Nation* (New York 1950); Jackson Turner Main, *The Antifederalists: Critics of the Constitution* (Chapel Hill, N.C., 1960); Forrest McDonald, *We the People: The Economic Origins of the Constitution* (Chicago 1958); Robert E. Brown, *Charles Beard and the Constitution: A Critical Analysis of "An Economic Interpretation of the Constitution"* (Princeton 1956); Jackson Turner Main, "Charles A. Beard and the Constitution: A Critical Review of Forrest McDonald's *We the People*," *William and Mary Quarterly* January 1960, 88–102, with a rebuttal by Forrest McDonald, ibid. 102–10.

3. See, e.g., Main, *Antifederalists* 280–81.

4. Cecelia Kenyon, "Men of Little Faith: The Anti-Federalists on the Nature of Representative Government," *William and Mary Quarterly* January 1955; Kenyon, "Introduction," *The Anti-Federalists* (Indianapolis 1966).

5. Gordon Wood, *The Creation of the American Republic, 1776–1787* (Chapel Hill, N.C., 1969) ch. 12. See Bernard Bailyn, *The Ideological Origins of the American Revolution* (Cambridge, Mass., 1967).

*6. For this reason "Anti-Federalist" seems the best rendering of the name. There was no consistent usage at the time and there has been none since. "Anti-Federalist" balances the positive and negative sides by giving the group (or the position) a proper name, while still emphasizing its character as opposition. The typographically convenient "Antifederalist," now generally in favor, suggests more cohesion than actually existed, while "anti-Federalist" suggests a merely negative, dependent unity. Forrest McDonald, apparently the only other writer to consider this little question in print, agrees about the implications of the main forms. He adopts "anti-Federalist" as "the more neutral term"; and while it is not neutral, it does accurately reflect his opinion, contrary to the conclusion here, that there was no significant theoretical coherence in the Anti-Federalist arguments or principles. Forrest McDonald, "The anti-Federalists, 1781–1789," *Wisconsin Magazine of History* Spring 1963, 206n.

7. Plebeian 6.11 and others.

*8. The fundamental unity of *The Federalist* can be disputed. See Douglass Adair, "The Authorship of the Disputed Federalist Papers" part 2, *William and Mary Quarterly* April and July 1944; repr. in Adair, *Fame and the Founding Fathers*, ed. H. Trevor Colbourn (New York 1974) 27–74. Alpheus Mason, "The Federalist—a Split Personality," *American Historical Review* LVII, no. 3 (1952). Gottfried Dietze, *The Federalist* (Baltimore 1960).

9. See Daniel Boorstin, *The Genius of American Politics* (Chicago 1953).

10. *The Federalist* no. 23, 151.

CHAPTER TWO

1. Brutus XIV, 2.9.184; [Maryland] Farmer I, 5.1.3; Martin 2.4.26; see Agrippa X, 4.6.43; XI, 4.6.47; XIV, 4.6.60; Monroe 5.21.37; Newport Man 4.25.1.

*2. "There is nothing solid or useful that is new—and I will venture to assert, that if every *political institution* is not fully explained by Aristotle, and other ancient writers, yet that, there is no *new* discovery in this the most important of all sciences, for ten centuries back." [Maryland] Farmer II, 5.1.21. In the exchange between A [Maryland] Farmer and his critic, Aristides, the former speaks in behalf of the older Anti-Federal heads against the rash, know-it-all Federalist youths. See Stanley Elkins and Eric McKitrick, "The Founding Fathers: Young Men of the Revolution," *Political Science Quarterly* LXXVI, no. 2 (1961).

3. Resolution of Congress, 21 February 1787, Farrand III, 14; [Pennsylvania] Farmer 3.14.22; Denatus 5.18.4; Henry 5.16.1; Columbian Patriot 4.28.4 (objections 16–18); Warren 6.4.38; Sydney 6.9.2, 7–8; Republican Federalist 4.13.5–7, 16; see Lansing and Paterson, Farrand I, 249–50 (16 June). See this volume, ch. 3 n. 17.

4. Martin 2.4.36; Lowndes 5.12.1; Republican Federalist 4.13.15 and passim. See also Federal Farmer II, 2.8.23; Republican Federalist 4.13.16; Delegate Who Has Catched Cold 5.19.13ff; Cornelius 4.10.15.

5. Centinel I, 2.7.4; Federal Farmer I, 2.8.1. See Smith 6.12.7 on the "fickleness and inconstancy" of a free people and the implications of that for governmental change. See Impartial Examiner 5.14.26; Countryman 6.7.8, 9; Warren 6.14.49–51.

6. *The Federalist* no. 78, 527. For an unusually radical Federalist statement of the right of the people to change their governments, see Conciliator to the Honest American, Philadelphia *Independent Gazetteer* 15 January 1788.

7. Henry 5.16.1.

8. G. Livingston, Elliot II, 287. Cf. Jensen, *The Articles of Confederation* ch. 1; Jensen, *New Nation*, conclusion; Vernon Parrington, *Main Currents in American Thought* (New York 1927–30) I, chs. 1, 2; III, pp. 410–11.

9. Lowndes 5.12.1; Philadelphiensis XI, 3.9.89; Denatus 5.18.14. See also Old Whig I, 3.3.3; Tredwell, Elliot II, 401.

10. Aristocrotis 3.16.17; Sidney, *New York Journal* 4 December 1888. See Isaac Q. Leake, *Memoir of the Life and Times of General John Lamb* (Albany 1850) 305–6; McDonald, *We the People* 113; McDonald, "The anti-Federalists," *Wisconsin Magazine of History* XLVI, no. 3 (1963); Main, *Antifederalists* xi–xii; Robert Rutland, *The Ordeal of the Constitution* (Norman, Okla., 1966) 5–6; Linda Grant DePauw, *The Eleventh Pillar: New York State and the Federal Constitution* (Ithaca, N.Y., 1966) 170–72. Federalist larceny on a much larger scale is a major theme of Wood's *Creation* (see p. 562).

11. [James Wilson] *Considerations on the Bank of North-America* (Philadelphia 1785) 19; Elliot III, 157; E. Wilder Spaulding, *New York in the Critical Period, 1783–1789* (New York 1932) 184. See Ford, *Essays* 412; Farrand I, 487 (30 June); Elliot IV, 281; Symmes 4.5.2; Henry 5.16. Federal Farmer IX, 2.8.116; XI, 2.8.143, 147; Kate Mason Rowland, *The Life of George Mason, 1725–1792* (1892) II, 190, 191; Monroe 5.21.12.

12. Burton A. Konkle, *George Bryan and the Constitution of Pennsylvania, 1731–1791* (Philadelphia 1922) 305.

*13. Main, *Antifederalists* xi. "Blush ye well meaning citizens, who have associated with such men as are the ringleaders of antifederalism (*alias* sedition) in the United States." A Patriotic Citizen, New Hampshire *Freeman's Oracle* 6 June 1788.

14. See the references to an "efficient federal government" by Federalists Rufus King, Nathaniel Gorham, and William Heath, Elliot II, 55–57, 69, 121.

15. Impartial Examiner 5.14.26.

16. See Candidus 4.9.23, 41, whose plan aimed at true federalism in both senses.

17. Albany Anti-Federal Committee 6.10.2; Pennsylvania Convention Minority 3.11.16–20; Smith 6.12.5; Plebeian 6.11.13; Warren 6.14.49; Philadelphiensis IX, 3.6.60; Gerry 2.1.4–5; Officer of the Late Continental Army 3.8.3; Agrippa III, 4.6.13; X, 4.6.43; [Pennsylvania] Farmer 3.14.18–21; Symmes 4.5.2; Brutus I, 2.9.5; Mason, Virginia ratifying convention, Elliot III, 29; Georgian 5.9.2–3; Martin 2.4 passim.

18. Farrand II, 667. See Republican Federalist 4.13.10; see extract of letter from William Pierce to St. George Tucker, 28 September 1787, *Gazette of the State of Georgia* 20 March 1788: "The great object of this new government is to consolidate the Union, and to give us the appearance and power of a nation."

19. *The Federalist* no. 85, 594. Cf. King, Elliot II, 55; Charles Pinckney, Elliot IV 255–56.

20. James Wilson, Farrand I, 413 (25 June); Demosthenes Minor, *Gazette of the State of Georgia* 15 November 1787.

21. Brutus I, 2.9.5.

22. Yates and Lansing 2.3.6.

23. Monroe 5.21.11; see Symmes 4.5.3; Federal Farmer I, 2.8.12–14.

24. Elliot II, 46. Cf. James Wilson in the Philadelphia ratifying convention, McMaster and Stone 263–64.

25. Farrand I, 166 (8 June); McMaster and Stone 227. Cf. similar arguments of A Citizen of America, Fabius, and David Ramsay, in Ford, *Pamphlets* 38, 55, 176–77, 373; A Citizen, *Carlisle Gazette* 24 October 1787; Plain Truth, McMaster and Stone 189.

26. See Farrand I, 166 (8 June); McMaster and Stone 301, 395; Elliot II, 445–47. Cf. Madison's draft of a preface to the Debates of the Constitutional Convention, Farrand III, 539ff; and a letter by William Pierce to St. George Tucker, dated 28 September 1787, *Gazette of the State of Georgia* 20 March 1788.

27. See Paterson, Farrand I, 259 (16 June); Clinton 6.13.16–18.

28. Agrippa VI, 4.6.24; XIII, 4.6.60. See, for the same view, Monroe 5.21.14; Lowndes 5.12.5; [Maryland] Farmer VII, 5.1.112.

*29. Whether there is some deeper basis of reconciliation of the parts of Wilson's argument need not be pursued here. Consider, however, his remarks to the Pennsylvania ratifying convention on 28 November 1787 to the effect that "to preserve the state governments unimpaired" was the "favorite object" of the framers; "and, perhaps, however proper it might be in itself, it is more difficult to defend the plan on account of the excessive caution used in that respect than from any other objection that has been offered here or elsewhere." McMaster and Stone 265. See Ralph Rossum, "The Political Pyramid and the Federal Republic: The Political Thought of James Wilson" (University of Chicago, Ph.D. diss. 1973). Cf. the interesting argument of Fabius (John Dickinson), Ford, *Pamphlets* 176–77.

30. Elliot III, 93–94; McMaster and Stone 322.

31. Centinel V, 2.7.99; Agrippa V, 4.6.21. See also Impartial Examiner 5.14.4; Officer of the Late Continental Army 3.8.3; One of the Common People 4.8.1; Martin 2.4.114; Pennsylvania House Minority 3.2.6–7; [Pennsylvania] Farmer 3.14.8. Cf. Hamilton's objection to divided sovereignty in Farrand I, 287 (18 June).

32. Ford, *Essays* 367–68. James Monroe was, as usual, more open to the Federalist view: "The mixture between the general and state governments, being partly a consolidated and partly a confederated one, suggests a balance between sovereignties that is new and interesting." He hoped that by drawing precise boundaries and establishing proper checks, it might survive. Monroe 5.31.36. See also this volume 34.

33. Henry 5.16.1. See the similar objections of Whitehill in Pennsylvania and Caldwell in North Carolina: McMaster and Stone 256–57; Elliot IV, 15–16, 23–24.

*34. Alexander Hamilton, Elliot II, 234. Also *The Federalist* no. 15, 93: "the evils we experience do not proceed from minute or partial imperfections, but from fundamental errors in the structure of the building which cannot be amended otherwise than by an alteration in the first principles and main pillars of the fabric."

*35. When it was argued by the Pennsylvania republicans in 1785 that the Bank of North America, established by Pennsylvania on the recommendation of Congress, should not be abolished without at least notifying Congress of the reasons for the repeal of the charter, Jonathan Dickinson Sergent replied with (according to Brunhouse) "characteristic Radical reasoning: 'We are not bound by any terms made by Congress—Congress are our creatures!' " Robert L. Brunhouse, *The Counter Revolution in Pennsylvania: 1776–1790* (Harrisburg, Pa., 1942) 175.

36. Farrand I, 250 (16 June).

37. Farrand I, 324 (19 June); see also ibid. 340–41 (20 June). See also Monroe 5.21.4ff; Martin 2.4.39; Henry 5.16.2; Massachusetts ratifying convention, Elliot II, 54–55 (King); Justice Chase in *Ware* v. *Hylton,* 3 Dall. 199, 224 (1798).

*38. Whether this is the true implication of the ratification provision is of course controversial; and some Federalists denied, or at least softened, this interpretation. Cf. the account in *The Federalist* no. 39, 253–54, with Chief Justice Marshall's interpretation in *McCulloch* v. *Maryland,* 4 Wheat. 403–5 (1819). And see the arguments of A Freeman, who was a Federalist, that the Constitution is the act of the people of the United States as several and separate sovereignties, *Pennsylvania Gazette* 23 January 1788.

*39. Again it can be argued that the ratification provision is based on federal principles, since the Constitution was to come into effect, when nine states had ratified, only as between the ratifying states. This equivocation is important, but, as the Anti-Federalists saw, the thrust is in the national direction. The underlying rationale is that the Union is the decisive political entity, as was very widely recognized on both sides at the time. Moreover the practical effect supports and underlines the theory. It is true that a state might decide to stay out of the new government. That that would be extremely difficult is less important than that a state could not alone prevent the others from making fundamental constitutional change, as it could under the Articles. That obviously alters the situation not only of a majority wanting to act but also of a minority wanting to block action. The practical effect of the nine-state ratification provision was to make not merely ratification but ratification by thirteen states more likely than it would have been under a thirteen-state ratification provision.

*40. General Charles Cotesworth Pinckney told the South Carolina House of Representatives: "The separate independence and individual sovereignty of the several states were never thought of by the enlightened band of patriots who framed this Declaration; the several states are not even mentioned by name in any part of it,—as if it was intended to impress this maxim on America, that our freedom and independence arose from our union, and that without it we could neither be free nor independent. Let us, then, consider all attempts to weaken this Union, by maintaining that each state is separately and individually independent, as a species of political heresy, which can never benefit us, but may bring on us the most serious distress." Elliot IV, 301–2. See Abraham Lincoln, Message to Congress in Special Session, 4 July 1861, *Collected Works* (ed. Basler) IV, 421–41. William W. Crosskey and William Jeffrey, Jr., *The Political Background of the Federal Convention* (Chicago 1980), the third volume of Crosskey's *Politics and the Constitution in the History of the United States* (vols. 1 and 2, Chicago 1953), is largely devoted to showing the primacy of the Union to the states, both in practice and in common opinion. Not all Federalists, however, took this view. See A Freeman, cited above, n. 38, and Thomas McKean, who described the new system as proposing a union of thirteen sovereign and independent states, McMaster and Stone 272. See also *Penhallow* v. *Doane,* 3 Dall. 54 (1795), where Justice Paterson took the view, contrary to Iredell, that external sovereignty never did belong to the states and that the sovereignty of the national government as to foreign relations was inherited from the Continental Congress. See *U.S.* v. *Curtis-Wright Export Co.,* U.S. 304 (1936), p. 299.

41. Elliot II, 158.

*42. After the Declaration of Independence the people "relaxed their union into a league of friendship between sovereign and independent states." State Soldier, *Virginia Independent Chronicle* 6 February 1788. "It was an honest and solemn covenant among our infant States, and virtue and common danger supplied its defects." A Citizen of Philadelphia, McMaster and Stone 106. See also Wilson, McMaster and Stone 226; Iredell, Elliot IV, 227; *Kent's Commentaries on American Law,* 12th ed., ed. O. W. Holmes, Jr. (Boston 1893) I, part 2, lect. 10, p. 212.

43. Resolution of Congress, 21 February 1787, Farrand III, 14.

*44. Farrand I, 253, 255 (16 June); 283 (18 June); 324 (19 June). See Elliot IV, 206, 215, 229. "The confederation had failed to answer the purposes for which governments are instituted among men. Its powers or its impotence operated to the destruction of those ends, which it is the object of government to promote." John Quincy Adams, *The Jubilee of the Constitution* (New York 1839) 65.

CHAPTER THREE

1. McMaster and Stone 287.
2. Henry 5.16.2.
3. Farrand I, 340–41 (20 June); see Brutus VII, 2.9.87.

*4. Hamilton himself confessed that "the extent of the Country to be governed, discouraged him." Farrand I, 287 (18 June); see also Wilson's account, McMaster and Stone 220ff. For arguments in defense of the small republic, this volume 16–21; Yates and Lansing 2.3.7; Brutus I, 2.9.11; Federal Farmer I, 2.8.14; IV, 2.8.75; XVII, 2.8.208; Sidney 6.8.1–2; Cato Uticensis 5.7.6; [Maryland] Farmer III, 5.1.52–53; Pennsylvania Convention Minority 3.11.16; Old Whig IV, 3.3.20; Monroe 5.21.13; Cato III, 2.6.12–13; Agrippa XII, 4.6.48; Albany Anti-Federal Committee 6.10.2; Centinel I, 2.7.19; V, 2.7.94; Martin 2.4.44; [Pennsylvania] Farmer 3.14.7, 9; Columbian Patriot 4.28.4; Warren 6.14.5; Smith 6.12.19–20; Henry 5.16.2; Clinton 6.13.13; etc.

5. Ellsworth, Farrand I, 406 (25 June); see Martin, Farrand II, 4 (14 July).

6. Federal Farmer II, 2.8.17; XII, 2.8.158; Cato III, 2.6.16; Impartial Examiner 5.14.6.

*7. In Gordon Wood's view, the Anti-Federalists became fervent defenders "of the traditional assumption that the state was a cohesive organic entity with a single homogeneous interest at the very time they were denying the consequences of this assumption." Wood understands this traditional view, the "republicanism" of the Revolution, to be a secularized Puritanism aimed at securing a sacrifice of individual interest to the common good. *Creation* 499, 418, and ch. 2. One of my own reasons for turning to the study of the Anti-Federalists was the expectation that they defended some such tradition; the Anti-Federalists seemed to be of interest as defenders of at least residual principles of premodern, preindustrial, preliberal worlds. Yet, without here taking up the more complex question of how far such principles may in fact have been involved in Revolutionary republicanism, they are strikingly absent from the Anti-Federalist thought. The Anti-Federalists are liberals—reluctant and traditional, indeed—in the decisive sense that they see the end of government as the security of individual liberty, not the promotion of virtue or the fostering of some organic common good. The security of liberty does require, in the Anti-Federalist view, the promotion of civic virtue and the subordination (not, in the usual case, "sacrifice") of individual interest to common good; but virtue and the common good are instrumental to individual liberty, and the resemblance to preliberal thought is superficial.

8. Farrand I, 49 (31 May).

*9. Federal Farmer III, 2.8.24. Agrippa XII, 4.6.50, referred to our present government, which "is respected from principles of affection and obeyed with alacrity." See Mason, Farrand I, 112 (4 June); Smith 6.12.10; Henry 5.16.17; Clinton 6.13.13.

10. Brutus I, 2.9.18.

*11. Richard Henry Lee, letter to ——, 28 April 1788, in Lee, *Letters* II, 464; Federal Farmer III, 2.8.24; VII, 2.8.93. One of the arguments for leaving the states to decide how they would raise the money needed by the general government was this need for popular confidence. "Because *each* being thus accommodated, and participating [in] the advantages of union,—*none* subjected to any inconvenience thereby,—all will consequently concur in nourishing an affection for the government, that so cemented them." Impartial Examiner 5.14.6.

*12. Agrippa XII, 4.6.48. See Cato III, 2.6.16; Pennsylvania Convention Minority 3.11.51; Brutus IX, 2.9.105–10; Candidus 4.9.23. If this thought seems utterly archaic, the modern reader may grasp it better by substituting "bureaucracy" for "standing army." The Anti-Federalists were not so much worried about military coups or about "militarism" in the popular sense, as about rigid rule of a large and varied republic by the force of government, of which the standing army is the ultimate expression. Consider Cato's challenge: "will you submit to be numbered like the slaves of an arbitrary despot; and what will be your reflections when the taxmaster thunders at your door for the duty on that light which is the bounty of heaven." VI, 2.6.41.

13. Cf. Brutus I, 2.9.14ff; IV, 2.9.45ff; [Maryland] Farmer VII, 5.1.98. Cf. James Wilson's remarks in the Constitutional Convention on representation with those in the Pennsylvania ratifying convention. Farrand I, 132–33 (6 June); McMaster and Stone 221ff. See Montesquieu, *The Spirit of Laws* XI, ch. 6.

14. Cf. Federal Farmer I, 2.8.4–6; VIII, 2.8.108; *The Federalist* no. 63; no. 74, 500; no. 76, 510–12; no. 79, 532.

15. Columbian Patriot 4.28.4; Pennsylvania Convention Minority 3.11.33–37; Tamony 5.11.7; Warren 6.14.8, 47; Symmes 4.5.7; Smith 6.12.9; Federal Farmer XIV, 2.8.178. Rotation was thought to serve not only as an instrument of responsibility but also as training in public service, thus contributing to the attachment of the citizens to their community. Smith 6.12.27–28.

16. Federal Farmer II, 2.8.15; Smith 6.12.15. See Brutus I, 2.9.14; III, 2.9.42; and passim; Pennsylvania Convention Minority 3.11.4–5; Martin 2.4.42; Clinton 6.13.35.

*17. The state legislatures "are so numerous as almost to be the people themselves. . . ." Federal Farmer XII, 2.8.163. See ibid. 2.8.155; VIII, 2.8.106; IX, 2.8.113; Smith 6.12.15, 22; Henry, Elliot III, 322; Lee 5.6.2.

18. Federal Farmer VII, 2.8.97.

*19. Federal Farmer XII, 2.8.158; see Centinel I, 2.7.3; VI, 2.7.106–10; IX, 2.7.129. "There are no such mighty talents necessary for government as some who pretend to them, without possessing them, would make us believe. Honest affections, and common qualifications, are sufficient. . . . Great abilities have generally, if not always, been employed to mislead the honest unwary multitude, and draw them out of the plain paths of public virtue and public good." [Trenchard], *Cato's Letters* I, 177–78, quoted by Friend to the Republic 4.23.8.

20. Federal Farmer IX, 2.8.113.

*21. There is a continuity in the argument, since the principle of representation, which is the cause of the difficulty, is generally admitted by the Anti-Federalists even in the small republic. Many of them did think that there is a quantitative limit to the reach of the representative principle, that that limit was exceeded by the dimensions of the United States, and that therefore any representative body covering the whole United States must be inherently inadequate and untrustworthy. See Federal Farmer VI, 2.8.75; VII, 2.8.99; Smith 6.12.9.

22. Smith 6.12.17–18; cf. Hamilton, Elliot II, 254–57.

23. Sydney 6.9.19. See [Maryland] Farmer III, 5.1.56–58.

*24. See this volume 41, 43–45. In addition, because of the dispersed circumstances of the landed interest it would not be equally represented under the new system, which would tend to follow the lead of the commercial interests. Cornelius 4.10.11.

*25. Federal Farmer XV, 2.8.190. A general verdict is one in which the jury finds either for the plaintiff or for the defendant in general terms, judging both law and fact, as opposed to a special verdict, in which a particular finding of fact is made by the jury, leaving to the court the application of the law to the facts thus found.

26. [Maryland] Farmer IV, 5.1.65; see generally ibid. 5.1.61ff.

*27. Federal Farmer XV, 2.8.190. Noah Webster argued, for example, that the trial of the vicinage was no longer necessary to do justice in individual cases. Ford, *Pamphlets* 53. However, the Federal Farmer made it clear that for him that was not the main concern.

*28. Smith 6.12.20; Federal Farmer V, 2.8.59. See [Maryland] Farmer III, 5.1.52; Turner in Massachusetts ratifying convention, Elliot II, 31; Smith 6.12.9; Agrippa XII, 4.6.48. While the Federalist writers were less concerned with this question, see A Federalist, *Boston Gazette and Country Journal* 3 December 1787, who denied an Anti-Federalist argument that a constitution maker should adapt the constitution to the pre-civil habits of the people: ". . . his object would be, to introduce a code of laws that would *induce* those habits of civilization and order, which must result *from* good government. The truth of the case is, that as a people, we are destitute of *Federal Features* and *Habits*—the several *State Constitutions* are *local, partial,* and *selfish;* they are not calculated in their construction to form *national views.* . . ."

29. Brutus I, 2.9.16.

30. Republican Federalist 4.13.26.

31. Agrippa IX, 4.6.34.

32. See Impartial Examiner 5.14.6; [Pennsylvania] Farmer 3.14.7.

33. Henry 5.16.8; cf. *The Federalist* no. 19, 122–23.

34. Cato IV, 2.6.27. See Friend to the Rights of the People 4.23.3; [Maryland] Farmer VII, 5.1.111; Turner 4.18.2; Columbian Patriot 4.28.1.

35. Federal Republican 3.6.21. See "The Congress under the New Constitution," *New York Journal* 28 January 1788; [New Hampshire] Farmer 4.17.4; Impartial Examiner 5.14.8.

36. See discussion of Agrippa, this volume 24, 25.

37. Turner 4.18.1. See Cato V, 2.6.34; Alfred 3.10.5; Lansing (New York), Elliot II, 218; Williams, Elliot II, 240; Warren 6.14 passim; Delegate Who Has Catched Cold 5.19.9. See Andrew Carnegie, *The Gospel of Wealth and Other Timely Essays* (1933), ed. Edward C. Kirkland (Cambridge, Mass., 1962) 3; Montesquieu, *The Spirit of Laws* XX, ch. 1.

*38. *Thoughts on Government,* John Adams, *Works* IV, 109. See Livingston, Elliot II, 341. Some of the Anti-Federalists for this reason favored sumptuary laws. See [Maryland] Farmer V, 5.1.82; George Mason, Farrand II, 344 (20 August), 606 (13 September). See this volume 75, 76 and ch. 4, n. 42.

39. Warren 6.14.157.

40. [Maryland] Farmer VI, 5.1.82; see Warren 6.14.132–33.

41. Delegate Who Has Catched Cold 5.19.16. See Federal Farmer XVI, 2.8.196, Henry 5.16.37; this volume, ch. 8.

42. R. H. Lee, letter to James Madison, 26 November 1784, Lee, *Letters* II, 304.

43. David 4.24.2.

44. See Clinton Rossiter, *Political Thought of the American Revolution* (New York 1963) 204–6. See Alexis de Tocqueville, *Democracy in America* I, part 1, ch. 9; II, part 2, chs. 15–19. Alan Aichinger, "Civic Education in the New Republic" (University of Chicago Ph.D. diss. 1970).

45. David 4.24 n.1. See the satire of Aristocrotis (3.16.3) describing the free-thinking origin of the Constitution as an attempt to deny any divine limits on civil rulers.

46. *Virginia Independent Chronicle* 31 October 1787. See Federal Republican 3.6.21.

47. Warren 6.14.148, 135–37. See Agrippa IX, 4.6.34; XII, 4.6.48. Also Federal Farmer IV, 2.8.53. American fears about American corruption are considered at length by Gordon Wood in *Creation* chs. 3 and 10.

*48. R. H. Lee, letter to James Madison, 26 November 1784, Lee, *Letters* II, 304. "William Penn" (Penn 3.12.18) found a contradiction in state constitutional provisions for liberty of conscience alongside provisions for religious oaths for office-holders; but he made no attempt to resolve it.

*49. See, for example, the remarks of Amos Singletary, Elliot II, 44. For a good statement of the Federalist case against test oaths (and civil religion in general), see A

Landholder (Oliver Ellsworth) in Ford, *Essays* 168–71, who, however, approved of "our laws against drunkenness, profane swearing, blasphemy, and professed atheism." See letter of William Williams, Ford, *Essays* 207–9.

50. Turner 4.18.2; see David Caldwell, Elliot IV, 199; Friend to the Rights of the People 4.23.3(9).

CHAPTER FOUR

1. Henry 5.16.6; Smith 6.12.2.

*2. See Madison's Notes of Proceedings of Congress, 21 February 1787; *Documentary History of the Constitution* IV, 80–81; see ibid. 22, 24–25; Luther Martin in the Constitutional Convention as favoring a dissolution of the Union in preference to any plan abandoning the equality of the states, Farrand I, 445 (28 June); II, 4 (14 July). While Patrick Henry and some other Anti-Federalists were widely thought to favor separate confederacies, their public statements described dissolution of the Union only as the lesser of evils. Main, in an appendix entitled "Separate Confederacies," concludes: "Possibly some of the Antifederalists favored the idea; however the evidence is very strong that most of the talk about separate confederacies was generated by the other side." *Antifederalists* 283–84. Main somewhat underestimates Anti-Federal support (equivocal as it surely was) for separation. See (in addition to the citations in Main) Lansing, Elliot II, 219; Smith, ibid. 382; Countryman 6.7.8; Sydney 6.9.2; Centinel XI, 2.7.140–42; Henry 5.16.8. The Federalists "generated" much of the talk about separate confederacies in 1787–88 because they thought it was the end to which the Anti-Federal opposition to the Constitution was, more or less deliberately, pointing. The Anti-Federalists' frequent denial of the capacity of any republican government to extend over such a wide territory as the United States left them open to the criticism of striking at the root of Union itself. (See Wilson, McMaster and Stone 386; Randolph, Elliot III, 71.) In attributing to the Anti-Federalists an *intention* to move toward separate confederacies, such Federalists as Publius were doubtless more than a little disingenuous. See *The Federalist* no. 1, 7; no. 2, 8; no. 2, 12; no. 59, 402; State Soldier, *Virginia Independent Chronicle* 6 February 1788; Ford, *Pamphlets* 81–82. Main indeed produces evidence to show that there was more support of separate confederacies among Federalists than among Anti-Federalists; but he does not make it sufficiently clear that the Federalist support of separate confederacies occurred prior to the proposed new Constitution. During the ratification debates the only support seems to have come from the other side. Previous to the appearance of the Constitution, separate confederacies were seen as means of strengthening bonds of interstate association. Thus Benjamin Rush wrote in October 1786 that "some of our enlightened men who begin to despair of a more complete union of the States in Congress" had secretly proposed three confederacies, each of which "they say will be united by nature, by interest, and by manners, and consequently they will be safe, agreeable and durable." Benjamin Rush to Richard Price, 27 October 1786, *Letters of Benjamin Rush*, ed. L. H. Butterfield (Princeton, 1951) I, 408. Once the proposed constitution was on the agenda, separate confederacies appeared rather as means of loosening interstate bonds.

*3. Jensen, *New Nation* xiv. But cf. the comment by Elbridge Gerry defending the report that was the basis of the "Great Compromise" in the Constitutional Convention: "We were neither the same Nation nor different Nations. We ought not therefore to pursue the one or the other of these ideas too closely." Farrand I, 532 (5 July).

*4. Where the Anti-Federalists used "nation," they nearly always meant the United States. Cato I, 2.6.4; III, 2.6.10, 18; Warren 6.14.21, 133, passim; [Maryland] Farmer III, 5.1.50–52 passim; Impartial Examiner 5.14.7; Plebeian 6.11.7, 23; Federal Farmer I, 2.8.10; etc. "Community" and "country" refer sometimes to the states, more often to the United States. Federal Farmer I, 2.8.6; II, 2.8.15; V, 2.8.61,62; IX, 2.8.113; Brutus I, 2.9.15; Brutus [Virginia] 5.15.1.

Patrick Henry's equivocal terminology is of a piece with his argument. While at least once he used "nation" in a context where it must refer to the state (Elliot III, 386), he began his first speech in the Virginia ratifying convention with a reference to "this great national [American] question," in the deliberations of which he regarded himself as the servant of the people of "this commonwealth" [Virginia]. He conceived "the republic" [probably Virginia] to be endangered and asked whether the existence of "the country" [probably the United States] was threatened. Elliot III, 21. Later he said he had come to preserve "the poor commonwealth of Virginia," and he appealed to "my beloved Americans" and the American spirit (5.16.2). He argued that "a majority of the community" [Virginia] has a right to alter the government (ibid.). "This country" [the United States] has not virtue enough to manage its own affairs (5.16.9). Epithets on "our country" [Virginia] are undeserved. Elliot III, 163.

5. Agrippa VIII, 4.6.31.

*6. Agrippa (VIII, 4.6.32) does not resolve the deeper question whether commerce is a unifying force within the states themselves, and in this he exhibits a characteristic Anti-Federal tension. On the one hand, he suggests that "the spirit of commerce is the great bond of union among citizens," presumably within as well as between states (I, 4.6.6). On the other hand, he is concerned to maintain a purity of population, morals, and religion that does not seem to be consistent with an open, vigorous commercial society. See for example, his criticism of Pennsylvania, VII, 4.6.26; cf. III, 4.6.12–13; Montesquieu, *The Spirit of Laws* XX, chs. 1–2.

7. Monroe 5.21.17.

8. *The Federalist* no. 15, 91–92.

*9. Citizen 6.5.4. "Like a person in the agonies of a violent disease, who is willing to swallow any medicine, that gives the faintest hope of relief; the people stood ready to receive the new constitution, in almost any form in which it could be presented to them," the Old Whig asserted, IV, 3.3.18.

10. McDonald, *We the People* 3. See Jensen, *New Nation* passim; Wood, *Creation* 393–94.

*11. Madison reported to Edmund Pendleton on 27 May 1787 that in general the members of the Convention "seem to accord in viewing our situation as peculiarly critical. . . ." *Documentary History of the Constitution* IV, 169; see ibid. 347; Ford, *Pamphlets* 369; A Landholder II, ibid. 142–45; *The Federalist* no. 37. See the oration of the youthful John Quincy Adams on 18 July 1787: "At this critical period, when the whole nation is groaning under the intolerable burden of these accumulated evils. . . ." *Columbian Magazine* September 1787.

12. Old Whig VI, 3.3.32; cf. *The Federalist* no. 15.

13. Federal Farmer I, 2.8.1.

14. Old Whig IV, 3.3.18; see Citizen 6.5.4.

*15. Federal Farmer VI, 2.8.70; Philadelphiensis II, 3.9.8–9; III, 3.9.17–18; Brutus I, 2.9.2; Candidus 4.9.5; Centinel I, 2.7.3.

A favorite target of those historians who doubt that the American difficulties in 1787 were as serious as they have been pictured is of course John Fiske's *The Critical Period of American History*, a popular version of what Merrill Jensen calls the "chaos and patriots to the rescue" view of the American Founding. "The point is," Jensen writes, "there were patriots on both sides of the issue, but . . . they differed as to desirable goals for the new nation. At the same time, of course, there were men as narrow and selfish on both sides as their political enemies said they were." *New Nation* xiii. The observation was anticipated and met by Publius; see *The Federalist* no. 1, 4–6; no. 37, 231–32.

16. See Smith 6.12.10.

17. Candidus 4.9.13.

18. Williams, Elliot II, 240.

19. Letter from Lee to George Mason, 15 May 1787, Lee, *Letters* II, 419. See Alfred 3.10.2; cf. Henry 5.16.20; Lansing, Elliot II, 218; Warren 6.14.14.

20. Candidus 4.9.18.

21. Alfred 3.10.5; Plebeian 6.11.22.

22. *The Federalist* no. 42, 279.

23. Henry 5.16.2; DeWitt 4.3.29; Alfred 3.10.2; Centinel I, 2.7.26; Warren 6.14.14, 125, 157; Citizen 6.5.4.

24. Elliot III, 358.

25. Farrand I, 110–14 (4 June).
26. Philadelphiensis III, 3.9.22; [Maryland] Farmer V, 5.1.75; see also Old Whig IV, 3.3.22.
*27. Henry 5.16.2. A Federalist writer in Albany asked the opponents "whether they imagine that the sounds of *public spirit* and DEMOCRACY will prove as effectual a charm in blunting the tomahawk and dagger, as they have been in lulling the senses and fears of the multitude." P. Valerius Agricola, *Albany Gazette* 6 December 1787.
28. Plebeian 6.11.12; Tredwell, Elliot II, 358; see Gerry 2.1.3, 8; Old Whig 3.3.18; Republican Federalist 4.13.25.
29. See this volume 111–12, references at Art. I, sec. 4.
30. See this volume 67–68.
31. Elliot III, 375.
32. State Soldier, *Virginia Independent Chronicle* 16 January 1788.
33. Hamilton, Elliot II, 351; Iredell, Elliot IV, 95; see also Gore, Elliot II, 66; Sedgwick, ibid. 96.
34. *The Federalist* no. 23, 151.
35. Symmes 4.5.20; see Clinton 6.13.5.
36. Widgery, Elliot II, 28; see also Turner 4.18.1; Elliot IV, 276.
37. [Maryland] Farmer II, 5.1.46.
38. Brutus VII, 2.9.90; cf. Federal Farmer XVIII, 2.8.215ff.
39. Smith 6.12.37; Plebeian 6.11.2; Cornelius 4.10.3; Old Whig IV, 3.3.38; Symmes 4.5.2.
40. Henry 5.16.23.
41. State Soldier, *Virginia Independent Chronicle* 6 February 1788; letter from a correspondent, ibid. 28 November 1787; see Freeholder, ibid. 9 April 1788.
*42. Henry 5.16.2 (toward end of speech). Cf. Madison, Elliot III, 135; Warren 6.14.121, 15, 23. In 1834 Andrew Jackson sought to persuade his fellow countrymen in his famous "Protest" that "it is not in a splendid government supported by powerful monopolies and aristocratical establishments that they will find happiness or their liberties protection, but in a plain system, void of pomp, protecting all and granting favors to none, dispensing its blessings, like the dews of Heaven, unseen and unfelt save in the freshness and beauty they contribute to produce." Andrew Jackson, "Protest," April 1834, James D. Richardson, *A Compilation of the Messages and Papers of the Presidents of the United States* III, 93.
43. Officer of the Late Continental Army 3.8.5; see Lee, *Letters* II, 464; Agrippa XI, 4.6.45; Aristocrotis 3.16.11.
44. Brutus VII, 2.9.87; cf. *The Federalist* no. 34.
45. Federal Farmer XVII, 2.8.213.
46. *The Federalist* no. 34, 211; cf. Brutus VIII, 2.9.96ff; etc.; but for a different Anti-Federal view, see Impartial Examiner 5.14.13–16.
47. [New Hampshire] Farmer 4.17.4.
48. Brutus VII, 2.9.86–87.
49. Brutus VI, 2.9.80.
50. See this volume 9–14. See Martin Diamond, "What the Framers Meant by Federalism," *A Nation of States,* ed. Robert A. Goldwin, 2d ed. (Chicago 1974).
51. See *The Federalist* no. 39; *McCulloch* v. *Maryland,* 4 Wheat. 316 (1819); James Wilson, McMaster and Stone 322.
52. *The Federalist* no. 9; but cf. no. 15.
53. Federal Farmer I, 2.8.10–11 and n. 9; VI, 2.8.72.
54. See this volume 15.
*55. The new federalism is anticipated in the Articles of Confederation in its attempt to secure the sovereignty of the states while also providing that the league shall be perpetual.
56. James Wilson, McMaster and Stone 229–31, 301–3; see Wood, *Creation* 524–32.
57. Elliot II, 195.
58. Monroe 5.21.17.
59. Agrippa VI, 4.6.23; see Henry 5.16.36.

*60. Henry 5.16.2. The power of the states to provide military training according to congressional discipline only meant that "the states are constituted drill sergeants and fuglemen to train up soldiers for the general government." Aristocrotis 3.16.11.

*61. Rufus King argued in Massachusetts that if the state legislatures found their delegates erring they could give them public instructions, which the senators would scarcely dare to ignore. Elliot II, 47. But while the Federal Farmer and other Anti-Federalists referred to the Senate as "representing 13 sovereign states" and as being organized "entirely on the federal plan" (Federal Farmer III, 2.8.28; XI, 2.8.143), others pointed out that the Senate was not in fact based on federal principles. The senators were elected by the state legislatures but were to vote as individuals and not as state delegates, and the implication surely was that, once elected, they were not mere delegates of the states. Countryman from Dutchess County 6.6.45. In fact, as a Pennsylvanian replied to James Wilson, the power to appoint means nothing without the power to control and dismiss. [Pennsylvania] Farmer 3.14.14–16. There was a considerable measure of disagreement among the Anti-Federalists on this whole issue; some opposed equal representation of the states in the Senate, others regarded it as the only good thing in the Constitution.

62. McMaster and Stone 264.

63. Federal Farmer XVII, 2.8.211.

64. Henry 5.16.16.

65. Ibid.

66. Farrand I, 286 (18 June).

67. [Pennsylvania] Farmer 3.14.8.

CHAPTER FIVE

1. Farrand I, 51 (31 May).

2. Ibid. 134 (6 June). Brackets indicate James Madison's revision; see C. J. Taney in *Ableman* v. *Booth*, 21 How. 506, 516 (1859).

*3. This leaves aside the additional and practically very powerful argument that the states were mostly larger than the traditional small republics anyway. See *The Federalist* no. 9, 52–53.

4. *The Federalist* no. 10, 57.

5. See Gordon Wood's excellent discussion of this point, *Creation* 409–13.

6. See Parrington, *Main Currents in American Political Thought* I, chs. 1, 2; III, pp. 401–3; Jensen, *New Nation* 424–27; Jensen, *The Articles of Confederation* passim; Wood, *Creation* 513.

7. See for example Farrand I, 51 (31 May), 288 (18 June); Elliot II, 10.

8. Letter from James Madison to Thomas Jefferson, 17 October 1788. Madison, *Writings* (ed. Hunt) V, 272.

9. Philadelphiensis X, 3.9.76.

10. Brutus IV, 2.9.45 and passim.

11. Clinton 6.13.2.

*12. "He had," Elbridge Gerry told his fellow delegates at Philadelphia, "been too republican heretofore: he was still however republican, but had been taught by experience the danger of the levilling spirit." Farrand I, 48 (31 May); see Mason, Farrand I, 101 (4 June).

13. James Burgh, *Political Disquisitions* (London 1774) I, 117. See Caroline Robbins, *The Eighteenth-Century Commonwealthman* (Cambridge, Mass., 1959).

*14. The difficult question of the franchise played little part in the ratification debate, since the Constitution left this matter to the states. While James Madison initially favored some form of freehold suffrage requirement as a way of checking the excesses of popular government, he later concluded that such a restriction on the franchise was dubious both in practice and in principle. See Farrand II, 203–4 (7 August) and Madison's very interesting fuller and more mature views in Farrand III, 450–55. See Wood, *Creation* 167–70.

15. Agrippa XVI, 4.6.73.

16. [Maryland] Farmer I, 5.1.15.

*17. Main, *Antifederalists* 173. Whether unmuted democratic views were as common as Main assumes even among the obscure people may well be questioned on the basis of the available evidence.

18. Wood, *Creation* 516.

*19. On the other hand, there were very few nondemocrats among the Federalists if by that is meant those who deny (1) that all powers derive from the consent of the governed and (2) that in general the will of the majority should prevail. Indeed, in his very important restoration of the thought of *The Federalist,* Martin Diamond insists on the Founders' "democratic" intentions. Martin Diamond, "Democracy and *The Federalist:* A Reconstruction of the Framers' Intent," *American Political Science Review* March 1959 (reprinted in Richard Stevens and Morton Frisch, *American Political Thought* [New York 1971]); "The Federalist," in *History of Political Philosophy,* ed. Leo Strauss and Joseph Cropsey, 2d ed. (Chicago 1972) 636–41. There is usage to support this view. Madison spoke in the Constitutional Convention of the need to remedy "the inconveniences of democracy" in ways "consistent with the democratic form of Govt." Farrand I, 135 (6 June). John Marshall said that the Federalists (in contrast to their opponents who had praised monarchy) "idolize democracy" and consider the Constitution to provide for "a well-regulated democracy." Elliot III, 222. Nathaniel Gorham asserted that the preponderance of the landed interest will enable it to prevent the introduction "of any other than a perfectly democratical form of government." Elliot II, 69. A Federalist essayist, A Patriotic Citizen, in New Hampshire (see above, ch. 2 n. 13) stressed that "the people are the sole, the great source from which all powers delegated to the federal government, by this truly democratic constitution, are to flow. . . ." See also [Pennsylvania] Farmer 3.14.2–3; Monroe 5.21 passim; Cato II, 2.6.8; Elliot II, 242; Penn 3.12.12. Nevertheless, while it is not inaccurate to say that the Founders favored a "well regulated democracy," to say that they favored "democracy" does not reflect dominant contemporary usage nor, I think, does it foster analytical clarity. The term "democracy" is ambiguous, containing a range of ideas from simple, direct popular rule to a regulated, checked, mitigated rule of the people. Generally, especially when aiming at precision of expression, both the Federalists and the Anti-Federalists used the term "popular government" to contain this whole range of ideas, reserving "democracy" for the former end of the scale and "republic" for the latter. See Elliot III, 394, and the very clear distinction drawn in *The Federalist* nos. 14 and 10. John Adams provides a good explanation in his *Defence* I, letter 3 (*Works* IV, 308–9).

*20. Henry 5.16.2. Cf. Federal Farmer V, 2.8.59; VII, 2.8.100. Cf. Madison, Elliot III, 87. On their side, the Federalists did not deny that rulers might be tyrannical, but they saw it as the secondary danger. But see the comment by Fabius (John Dickinson) that history "holds up the *licentiousness* of the people, and *turbulent temper* of some of the states, as *the only causes* to be dreaded, not the conspiracies of federal officers." Ford, *Pamphlets* 200. See this volume 50, 51.

21. See this volume, ch. 3.

22. Federal Farmer II, 2.8.23; see Brutus I, 2.9.18.

23. Cato III, 2.6.20.

*24. *The Federalist* no. 17, 107; italics added. See Elliot II, 354–55. Publius goes on to argue that this consideration is strengthened by the state's administration of ordinary criminal and civil justice, thus involving itself in the daily lives of the people.

*25. *The Federalist* no. 27, 172; italics added. Added to this consideration is the increased mingling of federal authority in the ordinary life of the people. Ibid. 173–74; no. 16, 102–3; cf. Plebeian 6.11.2.

Some of the Anti-Federalists saw the implication for the states of this line of argument. John Smilie thought that, for just such reasons as Publius gave, the people would become unwilling to support the state governments at all. "For, Sir, the attachment of citizens to their government and its laws is founded upon the benefits which they derive from them, and it will last no longer than the duration of the power to confer those benefits. When, therefore, the people of the respective States shall find their governments grown torpid, and divested of the means to promote their welfare and interests, they will not, Sir, vainly idolize a shadow, nor disburse their hard earned wealth without the prospect of a compensation. The constitution of the States having become weak and useless to every beneficial purpose, will be suffered to dwindle and decay, and thus if the governors of the Union are not too impatient for the accomplishment of unrivalled and absolute dominion, the destruction of State jurisdiction will be produced by its own insignificance." McMaster and Stone 270–71.

*26. Elliot II, 254. See Wilson, ibid. 474; Philadelphiensis X, 3.9.80: "The allegiance of freemen to government will ever be a consequence of protection."

27. Jasper Yeates, McMaster and Stone 298; cf. Charles Cotesworth Pinckney, John Marshall, Elliot III, 231; Tench Coxe, Ford, *Pamphlets* 147; John Dickinson, ibid. 174.

28. Elliot IV, 261, 260–61.

29. Edward Carrington to Thomas Jefferson, 9 June 1787, *Proceedings of the Massachusetts Historical Society* 2d series, XVII, 463.

30. Hamilton, Elliot II, 353; see Randolph, Elliot III, 84–85.

*31. *The Federalist* no. 63; cf. Montesquieu, *The Spirit of Laws* XI, ch. 6. Some Federalists did describe representation as a new idea. Thus Noah Webster asserted that "the moderns have invented the doctrine of *representation,* which seems to be the perfection of human government." Ford, *Pamphlets* 30, 42–43. See also Gorham, Elliot II, 68–69; Wilson, ibid. 423ff and McMaster and Stone 221ff.

32. State Soldier, *Virginia Independent Chronicle* 19 March 1788; cf. Ames, Elliot II, 8; *The Federalist* no. 10.

33. Henry 5.16.27; Smith 6.12.17.

*34. McMaster and Stone 335. The Pennsylvania Constitution of 1776 provided (II, sec. 7): "the house of representatives of the freemen of this commonwealth shall consist of persons most noted for wisdom and virtue, to be chosen by the freemen of every city and county of this commonwealth respectively." John Adams in his influential *Thoughts on Government* wrote of deputing power "from the many to a few of the most wise and good." *Works* IV, 194.

35. Livingston, Elliot II, 293; replied to by Smith, ibid. 310–11.

36. *The Federalist* no. 10, 62. Cassius (a Federalist reply to R. H. Lee), *Virginia Independent Chronicle* 2 April 1788; see Gouverneur Morris, Farrand II, 30–31 (17 July).

37. McMaster and Stone 336.

*38. Charles Cotesworth Pinckney, Elliot IV, 302. Consider, however, Hamilton's reflection that demagogues are not always petty men. Farrand I, 147 (6 June). Publius concedes that the the case is equivocal. If the large republic has a larger proportion of fit characters, it also has a larger proportion of bad ones; if corruption is more difficult, so is popular supervision of representatives. *The Federalist* no. 10, 63.

*39. *The Federalist* no. 57, 384. Nevertheless, it goes too far to say, as Gordon Wood does, that putting "good men into the administration" is "the crux of the Federalist argument," as indeed Wood's summary chapter sufficiently shows. *Creation* 508, 602–6. See this volume 53, 54, on limited government.

40. Ford, *Pamphlets* 40.

*41. Elliot II, 8. Wood sees behind such views the old notion of virtual representation based on an "organic" and homogeneous society, together with the clever rhetoric of a social elite seeking to maintain its position. The more plausible foundation is the ostensible one, the belief that even in a civil society devoted to the preservation of individual liberty, there is an objective collective interest which does not necessarily coincide with popular inclinations. Cf. Wood, *Creation* chs. 5, 12; *The Federalist* no. 71, 482–83.

42. Brutus I, 2.9.16; cf. Impartial Examiner 5.14.6.

43. *A Defence of the Constitutions of Government of the United States of America* I, letter 3 (John Adams, *Works* IV, 309–10). On citations to the *Defence,* see Martin 2.4.38 n. 9.

*44. Hamilton, Farrand II, 288 (18 June). See the very interesting discussion in [Carter Braxton] *An Address to the Convention of . . . Virginia . . . By a Native of that Colony* (Philadelphia 1776). Braxton describes the severe limits that a democratic regime based on public virtue requires. "Schemes like these may be practicable in countries so sterile by nature as to afford a scanty supply of the necessaries and none of the conveniences of life," but in a more bountiful country men "will always claim a right of using and enjoying the fruits of their honest industry, unrestrained by any ideal principles of government. . . These are rights which freemen will never consent to relinquish, and after fighting for deliverance from one species of tyranny, it would be unreasonable to expect they should tamely acquiesce under another" (p. 17).

45. Centinel VIII, 2.7.126; see also [New Hampshire] Farmer 4.17.8.

46. See Harry V. Jaffa, "Agrarian Virtue and Republican Freedom: An Historical Perspective," *Equality and Liberty: Theory and Practice in American Politics* (New York 1965).

*47. Ford, *Essays* 140. A Landholder explains to his readers that he is a merchant, now retired to the country—the best of both worlds, as it were. See also *The Federalist* no. 12, and cf. Charles Pinckney's different view, Elliot IV, 321–22.

48. Noah Webster, Ford, *Pamphlets* 59.

*49. See "Vices of the Political System of the U. States," April 1787, Madison, *Writings* (ed. Hunt) II, 366–69; Farrand I, 134–36 (6 June); *The Federalist* no. 10; letter to Thomas Jefferson, 24 October 1787, Madison, *Writings* (ed. Hunt) V, 17–41, esp. 32. Douglass Adair has shown that Charles Beard was largely responsible for initiating the present-day prominence of *The Federalist* no. 10 and for giving it a peculiar interpretation. Adair shows without difficulty that Beard's description of Madison's theory as a form of economic determinism is wrong. He also shows that Madison had carefully worked out his defense of the extended republic and that it had played a prominent role in Madison's argument in the Constitutional Convention. The influence of Madison's arguments or the role played, more broadly, by various versions of the notion of the extended republic are questions that have yet to receive satisfactory examination. Adair, "The Tenth Federalist Revisited," *William and Mary Quarterly* January 1951; " 'That Politics May Be Reduced to a Science': David Hume, James Madison and the Tenth Federalist," *Huntington Library Quarterly* August 1957; both articles reprinted in Adair, *Fame and the Founding Fathers* chs. 3, 4.

50. Farrand I, 136 (6 June).

51. Brutus I, 2.9.16; see Federal Farmer VIII, 2.8.110.

52. See Charles Pinckney, Elliot IV, 326–27; G. Morris, Farrand II, 54 (19 July).

53. Elisha Douglass, *Rebels and Democrats* (Chapel Hill, N.C., 1955) 148, quoting *American Archives* 4th series, III, 1514.

*54. See A Citizen of America [Noah Webster], Ford, *Pamphlets* 55–56. Nevertheless, the Federalists preached too, though relying on it less. See, for example, James Wilson's Fourth of July Address, *Boston Gazette and Country Journal* 28 July 1788; Ralph Lerner, "The Supreme Court as Republican Schoolmaster," *Supreme Court Review* 1967.

55. Letter from Thomas B. Wait to George Thatcher, 22 November 1787, "Thatcher Papers," *Historical Magazine* November 1869, 258.

CHAPTER SIX

1. Lincoln, Elliot IV, 313. See the characteristic argument made by John Dewitt 4.3.10–14; Centinel I, 2.7.5–24.

*2. See Wood, *Creation* 488–92 and 503. Wood, however, underestimates the extent to which what he describes as the Old Whig concern with a dichotomy between rulers and people is still an important part of the Anti-Federal concern with aristocracy.

*3. See Mason 2.2.3–4; Brutus XVI, 2.9.202–4; "The Congress" (see above, ch. 3 n. 35); Cincinnatus IV, 6.1.26–34; V, 6.1.36. See Madison on the debate on executive departments in the first Congress, *Annals of Congress* I, 380 (1 May): "Perhaps there was no argument urged with more success or more plausibly grounded against the Constitution, under which we are deliberating, than that found in the mingling of the

Executive and Legislative branches of the Government in one body." James Wilson confessed that the powers of the Senate were not favorite provisions of his but were generally desired. McMaster and Stone 326ff.

4. Cincinnatus V, 6.1.35; Centinel I, 2.7.23. See A Citizen, *Carlisle Gazette* 24 October 1787 (reply to Centinel).

5. Monroe 5.21.27; Federal Farmer XIV, 2.8.177; [Maryland] Farmer II, 5.1.30–31; "The Congress" (see above, ch. 3 n. 35); cf. Mason 2.2.6.

*6. Federal Farmer XIV, 2.8.178. Here again the Federal Farmer took the more traditional view, similar to Adams but different from Madison and from Publius. "In every large collection of people there must be a visible point serving as a common centre in the government, towards which to draw their eyes and attachments. The constitution must fix a man, or a congress of men, superior in the opinion of the people to the most popular man in the different parts of the community, else the people will be apt to divide and follow their respective leaders." Ibid. Cf. John Adams, *Defence* I, preface, letter 55 (*Works* IV, 285–92, 585). While A [Maryland] Farmer argued for the need in a representative system for an executive for life (V, 5.1.74), The Federal Farmer would have the executive limited to one several-year term. Both sought to avoid the convulsions invited by short-range terms and re-eligibility; rather than that, The Federal Farmer said, it would be "almost as well" to establish a hereditary executive (XIV, 2.8.180). Cf. Cornelius 4.10.12–15; Williamson, Farrand II, 101 (24 July); Franklin, Farrand I, 83 (2 June), 103 (4 June).

*7. Farrand I, 101–2, 113–14 (4 June). Randolph expressed himself as opposing "a unity in the Executive magistracy" which would be "the foetus of monarchy," a form of government altogether inconsistent with the fixed genius of the American people. Farrand I, 66 (1 June). See Centinel II, 2.7.51; Pennsylvania Convention Minority 3.11.45; Federal Republican 3.6.39; Maryland Convention Minority 5.4.7.

8. Mason, Elliot III, 496–97; Philadelphiensis IX, 3.9.61 (see also 3.9.57, 58, 60); Clinton 6.13.32; Cato IV, 2.6.25–26; Old Whig V, 3.3.31; Sidney 6.8.1; Officer of the Late Continental Army 3.8.3; Cornelius 4.10.12, 20–21; Lowndes 5.12.4; Impartial Examiner 5.14.38–40; Henry 5.16.7.

9. Symmes 4.5.2.

10. Henry 5.16.11.

11. Federal Republican 3.6.23–24; see Wilson, McMaster and Stone 359.

*12. On the Federalist side Charles Pinckney of South Carolina predicted that the national judiciary "might be made the keystone of the arch, the means of connecting and binding the whole together, of preserving uniformity in all the judicial proceedings of the Union. . . . [I]n republics, much more (in time of peace) would always depend upon the energy and integrity of the judicial than on any other part of the government—that, to insure these, extensive authorities were necessary. . . ." Elliot IV, 258.

13. Brutus XV, 2.9.186, 193. On judicial review, see also Centinel XVI, 2.7.168; Countryman from Dutchess County 6.6.27, 28; Martin 2.4.89; James Wilson, Elliot II, 489, 446, and McMaster and Stone 304–5; Ellsworth, Elliot II, 196.

*14. Federal Farmer XV, 2.8.185. Publius contended that "the judiciary, from the nature of its functions, will always be the least dangerous to the political rights of the constitution. . . . [T]hough individual oppression may now and then proceed from the courts of justice, the general liberty of the people can never be endangered from that quarter. . . ." *The Federalist* no. 78, 522–23.

15. Centinel V, 2.7.101.

*16. McMaster and Stone 280. Publius rejected this "political heresy," yet concluded that "the true test of a good government is its aptitude and tendency to produce a good administration." *The Federalist* no. 68, 461.

17. *The Federalist* no. 51, 349; R. R. Livingston, Elliot II, 345.

18. Demosthenes Minor, *Gazette of the State of Georgia* 15 November 1787 (see also his essay on 22 November 1787); Cassius, *Virginia Independent Chronicle* 2 April 1788.

19. Randolph, Elliot III, 70.

20. Iredell, Elliot IV, 221; see also ibid., 195: "There is a degree of jealousy which

it is impossible to satisfy." See McKean, McMaster and Stone 274–75; One of the Middle Interest, *Massachusetts Centinel* 28 November 1787.

21. Alfredus, New Hampshire *Freeman's Oracle* 18 January 1788.

22. *The Federalist* no. 76, 513–14.

*23. Agrippa XV, 4.6.71; Farrand II, 285 (14 August); see also Old Whig III, 3.3.17; Republican Federalist 4.13.18. See Thomas Jefferson, the Kentucky Resolutions: ". . . confidence is everywhere the parent of despotism—free government is founded in jealousy and not in confidence; it is jealousy, and not confidence which prescribes limited constitutions, to bind down those whom we are obliged to trust with power. . . ." *The Complete Jefferson,* ed. Saul K. Padover (New York 1943) 133. Samuel Adams: "[T]here is a Degree of Watchfulness over all Men possessed of Power or Influence upon which the Liberties of Mankind much depend." Letter to Elbridge Gerry, 23 April 1784, *The Writings of Samuel Adams,* ed. H. A. Cushing (New York 1904–8) IV, 302.

*24. Brutus IV, 2.9.54; Elliot II, 295–96; Smith 6.12.34. Cf. Federal Farmer III, 2.8.25; *The Federalist* no. 51, 349. The Anti-Federalists were impressed with Burgh's caution: "To take the character of man from history, he is a creature capable of any thing the most infernally cruel and horrid, when actuated by interest, or what is more powerful than interest, passion, and not in immediate fear of punishment from his fellow-creatures; for damnation lies out of sight. Who would trust such a mischievous monkey with superfluous power?" Burgh, *Political Disquisitions* I, 106. See N. Barrell in Elliot II, 159, and in letter to George Thatcher, 15 January 1788, *Historical Magazine* November 1869, 264–65; Columbian Patriot 4.28 passim; Luther Martin, Ford, *Essays* 378. And see Georgian 5.9.2: ". . . mankind, upon the whole, is so depraved as, with pleasure, to trample upon the sacred rights and privileges of their fellow creatures."

25. Federal Farmer IV, 2.8.58.

26. Centinel I, 2.7.9.

27. [Maryland] Farmer II, 5.1.30.

*28. Henry 5.16.14. "The executive branch of the government was eternally in action; it was ever awake; it never slept; its action was continuous and unceasing, like the tides of some mighty river, which continued flowing and flowing on, swelling, and deepening, and widening, in its onward progress, till it swept away every impediment, and broke down and removed every frail obstacle which might be set up to impede its course." Henry Clay, Speech on the Amendment of the Constitution Respecting the Veto Power, 24 January 1842, *Life and Speeches of The Hon. Henry Clay,* ed. Daniel Mallory, 4th ed. (New York 1844) II, 519. See Jefferson to Edward Carrington, 27 May 1788: "The natural progress of things is for liberty to yeild [*sic*] and government to gain ground." *The Papers of Thomas Jefferson,* ed. Julian P. Boyd (Princeton 1950–) XIII, 208–9.

CHAPTER SEVEN

1. See the very good statement by The Federal Farmer I, 2.8.13, and VI, 2.8.70.

2. Plebeian 6.11.12, 2.

3. Old Whig I, 3.3.3.

4. See this volume, ch. 6.

5. Elliot II, 348.

6. Henry, Elliot III, 579; see Cato III, 2.6.14.

7. Denatus 5.18.5.

8. Centinel IV, 2.7.89; G. Livingston, Elliot II, 388; Selected Committee for Cumberland County, *Carlisle Gazette* 5 March 1788; Columbian Patriot 4.28.4.

9. Henry 5.16.2.

10. Columbian Patriot 4.28.4. See Henry 5.16.11: "This Government is so new it wants a name."

11. Martin 2.4.38.

*12. Part of the limited character of the new government was the very division of power between the general government and the states, which has been discussed above (ch. 4). "Separation of powers" and "checks and balances" often took on an additional meaning for the Anti-Federalists, and even"mixed government" was sometimes used to refer to the "mixture" of general and state governments. Henry 5.16.22; Federal Farmer VI, 2.8.78. A major difficulty with the notion of a federal balance, however, is the absence of any third, "balancing" power. See Dickinson's excellent brief statement of the relation between traditional checks and balances and the American federal-state balance in the Constitutional Convention. Farrand I, 86–87 (2 June), 152–53 (7 June).

13. Kenyon, *The Antifederalists* lxxx.

14. See also Lowndes 5.12.3.

*15. The evidence bearing on the question of the influence on the Constitutional Convention of John Adams' book, the first volume of which reached Philadelphia in the spring of 1787, is slender. According to Charles Francis Adams, it "was much circulated in the convention, and undoubtedly contributed somewhat to give a direction to the opinions of the members." Benjamin Rush suggested to Richard Price that Adams' book was having a valuable effect on the constitutional deliberations. The influence has probably been exaggerated. As the text makes clear and as Gordon Wood has recently shown, the Constitutional scheme of complex government was quite different from Adams'. Yet they *were* both schemes of complex government. It is quite clear in any case that many Anti-Federalists took Adams' ideas to have been influential; and the *Defence* figured significantly in their discussions of the Constitution. John Adams, *Works* IV, 276; letter of Benjamin Rush to Richard Price, 2 June 1787, *Letters of Benjamin Rush* (ed. Butterfield) I, 418; Page Smith, *John Adams* (Garden City, N.Y., 1962) 698–701; Wood, *Creation* ch. 14; Centinel I, 2.7.7–9; Humble 3.7.1.

16. Centinel I, 2.7.7.

17. See *Defence*, preface (John Adams, *Works* IV, 284).

18. See *Defence*, letters 23, 25, 55 (John Adams, *Works* IV, 380–82, 397–98, 579–80.

*19. The American Founding generation found access to this tradition mainly, though by no means exclusively, through Montesquieu's *The Spirit of Laws* and William Blackstone's *Commentaries on the Laws of England*, each in its way a modern adaptation of old ideas of the mixed regime. An important early American statement is to be found in *The Essex Result* (Newbury-Port 1778), printed in Theophilus Parsons, Jr., *Memoir of Theophilus Parsons* (Boston 1859) 359 ff. Most secondary work on mixed government and the separation of powers has now been superseded by M. J. C. Vile, *Constitutionalism and the Separation of Powers* (Oxford 1967), and W. B. Gwyn, *The Meaning of the Separation of Powers* (New Orleans 1965).

20. Centinel I, 2.7.8–9. For a fuller and better argument in favor of simple government, see [anon.] *Four Letters on Interesting Subjects* (Pennsylvania 1776) (Evans, *Early American Imprints* no. 14759).

21. [Maryland] Farmer II, 5.1.34.

22. See this volume, ch. 6.

23. [Maryland] Farmer V, 5.1.69; see ibid. 80–82; Warren 6.14.168. See Adams' somewhat different account in his *Defence*, preface (*Works* IV, 289–90), and Monroe's in his *Some Observations* 5.21.21. On the obsolescence of pure democracy, see Alexis de Tocqueville, "Report Given before the Academy of Moral and Political Sciences on January 15, 1848 . . .," in *Democracy in America*, ed. Mayer (Garden City, N.Y., 1969), Appendix II, 740.

24. *Defence*, letter 25 (John Adams, *Works* IV, 397).

25. [Maryland] Farmer II, 5.1.29, 31.

26. Ibid. 5.1.18–49; V, 5.1.68–83.

*27. Henry 5.16.14. "There being nothing to prevent his [the President's] corruption but his virtue, which is but precarious, we have not sufficient security." Monroe, Elliot III, 489; see ibid. 218–19.

28. Henry 5.16.7, 14.

*29. Federal Farmer XI, 2.8.146, 145. It should be noted that The Federal Farmer's proposal was to increase the number in the Senate and to connect it with the states for stability and stature, so that his concern with a stronger place for the states in the new general government would also be served. See also ibid. VII, 2.8.97: "We talk of balance in the legislature, and among the departments of government; we ought to carry them to the body of the people."

*30. The same question arises in connection with the executive. Madison stated this in the convention on 6 June when he referred to the difficulty of rendering the executive competent to its own defense in a republic, "which could not give to an individual citizen that settled pre-eminence in the eyes of the rest, that weight of property, that personal interest against betraying the National Interest, which appertains to an hereditary magistrate." Farrand I, 138. See The Federalist nos. 76–77.

*31. Noah Webster, defending the need for a senate, even though there was no American nobility, said that "in most of our American constitutions, we have all the advantages of checks and balances, without the danger which may arise from a superior and independent order of men." Ford, Pamphlets 35ff.

*32. Elliot III, 218–19. See also the similar observation of A Citizen in the Carlisle Gazette for 24 October 1787, who contended that the branches were not intended to balance one another (at least, it may be added, not in the Adams sense) as Centinel claimed: "The sole intention of it is to produce wise and mature deliberations."

33. Officer of the Late Continental Army 3.8.3.

34. Centinel II, 2.7.50; Brutus XVI, 2.9.197.

*35. Federal Farmer X, 2.8.135. The writer went on to say, "and all be conformable to the condition of the several orders of the people," which is an additional part of the argument considered above. See also ibid. XIV, 2.8.173–78; Adams, Defence, letter 55 (Works IV, 581–84); Blackstone, Commentaries on the Laws of England I, 48–52. Cf. the scheme in Tussman and tenBrock, "The Equal Protection of the Laws," California Law Review September 1949; and Vile, Constitutionalism and the Separation of Powers ch. 1.

*36. This is fundamentally the same argument made for an independent national executive as a result of experience under the Articles of Confederation. See Charles Thach, The Creation of the Presidency, 1775–1789: A Study in Constitutional History (Baltimore 1922) ch. 3. The position is compatible with legislative supremacy; and it was held by the civil service reformers of the late nineteenth century, who argued in favor of the independence of the civil service, even against the legislature, precisely on the ground that this was the only way the civil service could efficiently serve the legislature.

37. The Federalist no. 48, 332.

*38. See the very interesting discussion by Brutus of this question in his last essay (XVI, 2.9.197ff). It is perhaps significant that the Brutus essays broke off before reaching the promised discussion of the senatorial power of impeachment—the critical case of a mixture of powers in behalf of popular responsibility.

39. This is what Publius explained in The Federalist nos. 47 and 48.

*40. ". . . it is impracticable, perhaps, to maintain a perfect distinction between these several departments—for it is difficult, if not impossible, to call to account the several officers in government, without in some degree mixing the legislative and judicial." Brutus XVI, 2.9.197; see also ibid. 202–3.

*41. This is the traditional view of balanced government; cf. this volume, 55–56.

*42. A Citizen, Carlisle Gazette 24 October 1787. See Pelatiah Webster's defense of the division of the legislature into three branches, to promote both safety and mature deliberation. The veto of the President "will furnish all the new light which a most serious discussion in a third House can give, and will make a new discussion necessary in each of the other two, where every member will have an opportunity to revise his opinion, to correct his arguments, and bring his judgment to the greatest maturity possible." "Remarks on the Address of the Sixteen Members . . . ," McMaster and Stone 96. See Jean Louis DeLolme, Constitution of England (London 1853) II, ch. 3, 156–62.

*43. Blackstone, Commentaries on the Laws of England I, 48–52; see this volume

55–56 and ch. 7 n. 17. The movement from Adams to Madison is, among other things, a movement from legislative sovereignty to constitutional balance.

*44. The three-part division of functions, legislative, executive, and judiciary, seems a natural basis for a three-part balance of power arrangement. We need not here inquire into the deeper implications of the question whether a balance of power system necessarily reduces itself in principle to a three-part system. A three-part balance of power, however fluid and complex, seems the obvious foundation for the constitution-maker and was so viewed by the men of the Founding generation. (A major difficulty of the "federal" system as a balance of power system is its lack of a third, "balancing," power.) Neither do our present purposes require a consideration of the important question of the status of the particular threefold division of functions that finds expression in the American constitution. The chief alternatives to this scheme are the legislative-federative-executive division of Locke and the simpler legislative-executive scheme occasionally favored in the late eighteenth century and later adopted by civil service reformers and students of public administration.

*45. Elliot II, 434; cf. McMaster and Stone 230–31. Later Wilson explained: ". . . all authority of every kind *is derived by* REPRESENTATION *from the* PEOPLE *and the* DEMOCRATIC *principle is* carried into every part of the government." James Wilson, ibid. 344. The Constitution "unites in its different parts all the advantages, without any of the disadvantages, of three well-known forms of government and yet it preserves the attributes of a republic." One of the Four Thousand, ibid., 116. If Europe has the merit of discovering representation, Publius said, "America can claim the merit of making the discovery the basis of unmixed and extensive republics." *The Federalist* no. 14, 84. See Wood, *Creation* 584.

*46. Some of the Federalists also had doubts, most notably Alexander Hamilton, who expressed in the Philadelphia Convention his doubts about the scheme in which "a democratic assembly is to be checked by a democratic senate, and both these by a democratic chief magistrate." Farrand I, 310 (18 June).

CHAPTER EIGHT

1. See this volume 22–23 for a discussion of the Anti-Federalists' view of religion.

*2. Pennsylvania Convention Minority 3.11.13. Many Anti-Federalists, especially in Pennsylvania, deplored the absence of any constitutional exemption from military service for conscientious objectors, such as the Quakers had enjoyed in Pennsylvania. Philadelphiensis II, 3.9.11.

*3. Cincinnatus I, 6.1.19. Others, on the other hand, were concerned that the officeholding could not be confined to Protestants or even Christians. Philadelphiensis II, 3.9.13.

4. Old Whig V, 3.3.27.

*5. The Anti-Federalists were especially warm in their defense of a free press, because of their own attempts to use the press to mobilize opinion in opposition to the Constitution and their belief that, in one way or another, attempts were being made to muzzle them. See below, Centinel II, 2.7.28–38. But they were also concerned, more deeply, that the Federalist lack of protection for a vigorous free press signaled a basic hostility to popular enlightenment, based on a dogma that government is too important a business for the people to be involved in. See Aristocrotis 3.16.3; Old Whig I, 3.3.3.

*6. Centinel I, 2.7.25; A Confederationist, *Pennsylvania Herald and General Advertiser* 27 October 1787. The precise meaning of freedom of the press was seldom discussed. James Wilson made the then-standard argument that it does not preclude the punishment of libel, including seditious libel: "what is meant by the liberty of the press is, that there should be no antecedent restraint upon it; but that every author is responsible when he attacks the security or welfare of the government or the safety, character and property of the individual." McMaster and Stone 308–9. See One of the Middle Interest (above, ch. 6 n. 20). Most of the Anti-Federalists would probably have accepted this understanding (see [New Hampshire] Farmer 4.17.3), but a few denied it, adopting the more modern view. A Confederationist went on to say, "When this declaration [of the liberty of the press] be made, let the attorney general of the United States, file an information against me for libel; I will carry that declaration in my hand, as my shield and my constitutional defence."

7. New Hampshire *Freeman's Oracle* 18 January 1788; Luther Martin, Ford, *Essays* 364–65; cf. James Wilson's federal liberty argument, this volume 11. See Remarker, *Boston Independent Chronicle* 22 December 1787.

8. McMaster and Stone 143–44; see Charles Pinckney, Elliot IV, 259–60; Agrippa XIII, 4.6.60.

9. McMaster and Stone 144, 354; see ibid. 304–5.

10. See Leonard Levy, *A Legacy of Suppression* (Cambridge, Mass., 1960).

11. Brutus II, 2.9.26; see ibid. 2.9.31.

12. Aristocrotis 3.16.15. Cf. Symmes 4.5.2 on the laconic character of the Constitution.

13. Old Whig II, 3.3.12. See [Maryland] Farmer I, 5.1.15.

14. Randolph, Elliot III, 464–65. See also Yeates in the Pennsylvania ratifying convention, McMaster and Stone 296.

15. Agrippa VI, 4.6.22; see Brutus II, 2.9.31; Henry 5.16.34–37; [Maryland] Farmer I, 5.1.12; Friend to the Rights of the People 4.23.6. For Federalist arguments being rebutted here, see Alfredus (above, ch. 6 n. 21); One of the Middle Interest (above, ch. 6 n. 20); A Citizen (above, ch. 2 n. 25); Civis Rusticus, *Virginia Independent Chronicle* 30 January 1788; Sherman, Farrand II, 588 (12 September).

16. Henry 5.16.37. Wilson, McMaster and Stone 254. See above, n. 12. See letter from S. Lee to George Thatcher, 19 January 1788, *Historical Magazine* November 1869, 266–67.

17. Federal Republican 3.6.50.

18. Samuel Chase, letter to John Lamb, 13 June 1788, in Leake, *Memoir of the Life and Times of General John Lamb* 310; see Philadelphiensis 3.9.43.

19. Impartial Examiner 5.14.4.

20. Brutus II, 2.9.24.

21. McMaster and Stone 252; see Wilson, ibid. 253–54.

22. Elliot III, 191.

23. A Native of Virginia [Burwell Starkes?], *Observations upon the Proposed Plan of Government* (Petersburg, Va., 1788); this pamphlet was at one time erroneously attributed to James Monroe and is printed in *The Writings of James Monroe*, ed. S. M. Hamilton (New York 1898–1903) I, 349–55. See Wilson, McMaster and Stone 252–54; One of the Middle Interest (above, ch. 6. n. 20).

24. McMaster and Stone 295. See also Cassius, Ford, *Essays* 28; Plain Truth, McMaster and Stone 190–91.

25. Remarker, *Boston Independent Chronicle* 27 December 1787.

26. Agrippa XVI, 4.6.73; see this volume 40.

27. Hamilton, Elliot II, 239; see Smith 6.12.20 n. 21, and Elliot II, 354–55.

*28. Federal Farmer IX, 2.8.121. Agrippa XV, 4.6.71: "But for want of a bill of rights the resistance is always by the principles of their government, a rebellion which nothing but success can justify."

*29. Brutus X, 2.9.128; see VI, 2.9.69. Luther Martin contended that a man might find himself compelled to be guilty of treason against the general government or against his state, when the latter is resisting the arbitrary encroachments of the former. Martin 2.4.96.

*30. *The Federalist* no. 28, 179. It is striking that Publius' reference to checks by the states on the general government are usually connected with some reference to the ultimate defense by the people of their rights. See *The Federalist* no. 26, 169; no. 46, 321–22; no. 60, 404.

*31. "The public good, in which the private is necessarily involved, might be hurt by too particular an enumeration; and the private good could suffer no injury from a deficient enumeration, because Congress could not injure the rights of private citizens without injuring their own. . . ." Bowdoin, Elliot II, 87–88.

32. Delegate Who Has Catched Cold 5.19.16; Old Whig IV, 3.3.22. See Impartial Examiner 5.14.10.
33. Federal Farmer XVI, 2.8.196.
34. Sec. 15. In Thorpe, *Federal and State Constitutions* 3814.

CHAPTER NINE

1. Pendleton, Elliot III, 37; cf. Nicholas, ibid. 98; State Soldier, *Virginia Independent Chronicle* 12 March 1788.
*2. Hamilton, Elliot II, 301. Similarly, cheap government is not necessarily good government. See Noah Webster, Ford, *Pamphlets* 47; also Oliver Ellsworth's formulation: "The cheapest form of government is not always the best, for parsimony, though it spends little, generally gains nothing. Neither is that the best government which imposes the least restraint on its subjects; for the benefit of having others restrained may be greater than the disadvantage of being restrained ourselves. That is the best form of government which returns the greatest number of advantages in proportion to the disadvantages with which it is attended." The Landholder, Ford, *Essays* 192. See A Native of Virginia (above, ch. 8 n. 23), in *The Writings of James Monroe* 352; Impartial Examiner 5.14.2.
3. John Jay, Ford, *Pamphlets* 71.
4. *The Federalist* no. 51, 349.
5. McMaster and Stone 351.
*6. Maecenas, *State Gazette of South Carolina* 6 December 1787. "What the government may terminate in depends on the people. . . . " Civis Rusticus, *Virginia Independent Chronicle* 30 January 1788, reply to Mason: ". . . the liberties of the people never can be lost, until they are lost to themselves, in a vicious disregard of their dearest interests, a sottish indolence, a wild licentiousness, a dissoluteness of morals, and a contempt of all virtue." Ibid. See Governor Huntington, Elliot II, 199–200.
7. Elliot III, 536–37.
8. *The Federalist* no. 55, 378; cf. no. 76, 513–14.
*9. For a revealing picture of Federalist government to contrast with Federalist principles of government, see Leonard D. White, *The Federalists* (New York 1948) chs. 2, 3, 8, 9, and 40, and *The Jeffersonians* (New York 1951) chs. 3–5 and 35.
*10. Cato V, 2.6.34. "Where then is our republicanism to be found? Not in our constitution but merely in the spirit of our people. That would oblige even a despot to govern us republicanly." *Memoirs, Correspondence and Miscellanies from the Papers of Thomas Jefferson,* ed. Thomas Jefferson Randolph, 2d ed. (Boston 1830) IV, 287.
11. *The Spirit of Laws* IV, ch. 5.
12. Federal Republican 3.6.21.
13. 1 Cranch 137, 176–78 (1803).
*14. *The Federalist* no. 49, 340–41. Cf. Madison to Jefferson, 4 February 1798, Madison, *Writings* (ed. Hunt) V, 438–39. John Marshall described the adoption of the Constitution as "a very great exertion." *Marbury* v. *Madison*, 1 Cranch 137, 176 (1803).
15. *The Federalist* no. 37, 238.
16. [John Dickinson] "Letter from a Farmer in Pennsylvania to the Inhabitants of the British Colonies" (1767), in *Empire and Nation,* ed. Forrest McDonald (Englewood Cliffs, N.J., 1962) 69. See *The Federalist* no. 37; A Citizen of New York [John Jay], "An Address to the People of the State of New York," Ford, *Pamphlets* 69–86.
*17. Impartial Examiner 5.14.15. See Mercy Warren, this volume 76. After the Revolution, Federalist John Jay wrote, "the spirit of private gain expelled the spirit of public good, and men became more intent on the means of enriching and aggrandizing themselves than of enriching and aggrandizing their country." Ford, *Pamphlets* 70–71; see Jay in New York convention, Elliot II, 284. Columbian Patriot 4.28.3:

"But there are certain seasons in the course of human affairs, when Genius, Virtue, and Patriotism, seems to nod over the vices of the times, and perhaps never more remarkably, than at the present period."

18. Lincoln, *Collected Works* I, 108–15. See Harry V. Jaffa, *Crisis of the House Divided* (Garden City, N.Y., 1959) ch. 9.

19. Columbian Patriot 4.28.12; see Mercy Warren on Washington, 6.14.54–77.

*20. The Federalists were not, generally speaking, less antislavery than the Anti-Federalists (indeed, one of the very few attempts to provide any kind of moral justification of slavery was made by Anti-Federalist Rawlins Lowndes); but their commitment to a policy of interest made it relatively easy to say, as did Oliver Ellsworth of the participation by the Southern states in the slave trade, that "their consciences are their own, tho' their wealth and strength are blended with ours." The Landholder, Ford, *Essays* 164; see also William Heath, Elliot II, 115. See Ford, *Pamphlets* 146; Martin 2.4.45, 68–70. The Anti-Federalists were less easily persuaded that questions of politics can be freed from questions of conscience.

21. Warren 6.14.67.

Appendix
Contents of the Complete Anti-Federalist

Appendix

VOLUME THREE

Pennsylvania

Introduction

Appendix

Volume Four

Massachusetts and New England

Introduction

VOLUME FIVE

PART 1

Maryland

PART 2

Virginia and the South

VOLUME SIX

PART I

New York

Appendix

PART 2

Conclusion

VOLUME SEVEN

Index

Index

Adair, Douglass, 92 n. 49
Adams, John: discussion of balanced government by, 55–56; on example of San Marino, 45; influence of on Constitutional Convention, 95 n. 15; on sources of inequality, 57
Adams, John Quincy, 83 n. 44
administration, Federalist emphasis on, 41–42, 51
Agricola, P. Valerius, 88 n. 27
agriculture, 45–46
Agrippa (pseud.), 11–12; attitude of toward commerce, 24, 25, 87 n. 6; on bill of rights, 40; on immigration policy, 19–20; on minority rights, 68; rejection of consolidation by, 24–25
Alfredus (pseud.), 64
amendments, 53
amendments, recommendatory, 36
America, remedy for ills of, 82 n. 34
American people, defense of liberty by, 72–73
American Revolution: influence of, 71; principles of, 8
Ames, Fisher, 11, 13
Annapolis convention, 9
Anti-Federalist (name), 9–10, 79 n. 6
Anti-Federalists: alleged faintheartedness of, 6; attitude of toward slavery, 100 n. 20; conservatism of, 7, 8, 22, 59; emphasis of on America's security, 27; jealousy of rulers, 51–52; lack of agreement among, 5; liberalism of, 83 n. 7; points of agreement with Federalists, 5; reassessment of, 3–4; role of in founding process, 3; separate confederacies and, 86 n. 2; traditional view of, 3–4; and Union, 86 n. 2; views of on representation, 44–45; weakness of their arguments, 71–72
Anti-Federalist thought: basic dilemma of, 6; development of, 32
aristocracy, natural, 17; Federalist view of, 44; [Maryland] Farmer on control of, 57–58
Aristocrotis (pseud.), 66

Aristotle, 80 n. 2
Articles of Confederation: Anti-Federalists on inadequacies of, 28; basic flaw of, 71–72; embodiment of principles of Revolution, 8; violation of by Constitutional Convention, 7
atheists, 22
avarice, Federalist reliance on in government, 48

balance, constitutional, 62
balanced government, 55–56, 59–60. See also mixed government
Beard, Charles, 92 n. 49
Beardian critique, 3–4
bill of rights, 3; Agrippa and [Maryland] Farmer on, 40; Anti-Federalists and, 64–70; educative function of, 21; possible dangers of, 67, 69
bills of rights, state, 66–67
blasphemy, 85–86 n. 49
Braxton, Carter, 91–92 n. 44
Brutus (pseud.): on homogeneity in republics, 45, 47; on reservation of rights, 67–68, 70; on need to restrain federal power, 66; on Supreme Court, 50; on tyranny, 39; theoretical importance of, 6
Bryan, George, 9–10
Burgh, James, 39–40, 94 n. 24

Candidus (pseud.), 26–27
Cassius (pseud.), 51
Centinel (pseud.), 50–51; attack of on checks and balances, 55; on freedom of press, 64; on separation of powers, 60, 61
Chase, Samuel, 67
checks and balances, 54–56, 58–59
Citizen (pseud.), 87 n. 9, 96 n. 32
citizenry, republican, characteristics of, 19–20
civil service, 96 n. 36
Civil War crisis, 76
Civis Rusticus (pseud.), 99 n. 6
Clay, Henry, 94 n. 6

Index

Clinton, George, 39
coercion: role of in government, 42–43
commerce, Anti-Federalist attitude toward, 20–21, 87 n. 6
commerce, promotion of, 30–31
common law principles, 66–67
Commonwealthmen, 39
community, in Anti-Federalist thought, 86 n. 4
confederacies, separate (partial), 24; Federalists and Anti-Federalists on, 86 n. 2
confederation, failure of, 83 n. 44
confederations (confederacies), 12
confidence in government, 84 n. 11
Congress. *See* legislature; House of Representatives; Senate
conscientious objectors, 97 n. 2
conservatism, Anti-Federalists and, 7, 22, 59
consolidated government, 65
consolidation, 10–11
constitution, British, 58
Constitution, federal: aristocratic character of, 48–52; founding generation's view of, 3; human qualities fostered by, 73; incoherence of, 54; novel features of, 97 n. 45; partly national, partly federal character of, 11–12; questions settled by, 3
Constitutional Convention, federal, 7
constitutions, state, 65
contradictions, Anti-Federalist attempts to reconcile, 6
conventions, state, 7
country, Anti-Federalist use of word, 86–87 n. 4
Countryman from Dutchess County (pseud.), 89 n. 61
Coxe, Tench, 6
critical period, 26, 87 n. 11, 87 n. 15

Declaration of Independence, 7
defense, national, 30–31
deliberation, wise, separation of powers and, 61
democracy, 39, 90 n. 19
democrats, Anti-Federalists as, 40
despotism, 51
Dickinson, John (Fabius), 90 n. 20
dictatorship, 49
divide et impera, Federalist application of, 47
drunkenness, 85–86 n. 49

education, 21
Elihu (pseud.), 22
Ellsworth, Oliver, 34, 99 n. 2
enumeration, 98 n. 30
executive power, 49, 94 n. 28

Fabius (John Dickinson), 90 n. 20
faction, majority, 41, 68
federal (word), ambiguity of, 9, 33
Federal Farmer (pseud.), 41, 93 n. 6; on bills of rights, 70; on federal legislature, 58–59; on government's duty to encourage best in people, 19; on happiness of people, 31; on judiciary, 50; on people's confidence in government, 16; on presidency, 49; on Senate, 96 n. 29; shift of from old to new federalism, 33; theoretical importance of, 6
federal government, 32
federal government, old, 54. *See also* Confederation
federalism, 7, 9
federalism, new, 33–34, 36–38, 88 n. 55
Federalist (name), 9–10
Federalist (pseud.), 85 n. 28
Federalist, The, 72–74, 82 n. 34, 82 n. 38, 92 n. 49. *See also* Publius
Federalists: attitude of toward slavery, 100 n. 20; Beardian view of, 3–4; confidence of in rulers, 50–51; degree of agreement among, 5–6; points of agreement with Anti-Federalists, 5–6; and separate confederacies, 86 n. 2; views of on democracy, 90 n. 19; views of on representation, 43–45
Fiske, John, 87 n. 15
force, as alternative to persuasion in government, 16–17
foreign influence, Anti-Federalist hostility to, 20
Founding Fathers, Anti-Federalists' place among, 3
Framers, disregard of legality by, 7–8
franchise, 89 n. 14
functions, separation of, 60–63

Georgian (pseud.), 94 n. 24
Gerry, Elbridge, 51, 86 n. 3, 89 n. 12
Gorham, Nathaniel, 90 n. 19
government: effect of on character of citizens, 19; Federalists' positive attitude toward, 71
government, limited. *See* limited government, doctrine of
government, science of, 80 n. 2
Grayson, William, 29
greatness, national, 30–31

habeas corpus benefits, 66
Hamilton, Alexander, 83 n. 4; on checks and balances, 54; on democratic nature of proposed government, 97 n. 46; on effective administration, 41–42; on large republics, 91 n. 38; on offensive war, 31
Henry, Patrick, 8, 20, 27, 30, 31, 35, 52;